Transforming Women's Education

The History of Women's Studies in the University of Wisconsin System

A Collaborative Project of

The University of

Wisconsin System

Women's Studies Consortium

Published by the Office of University Publications for
the University of Wisconsin System Women's Studies Consortium
1660 Van Hise Hall
1220 Linden Drive
Madison, WI 53706

Distributed by the University of Wisconsin Press, Madison, Wisconsin
www.wisc.edu/wisconsinpress/

Contents

Acknowledgments

Laura Stempel Mumford

L ike the women's studies programs its narrative describes, this book is the result of a collaborative effort among women throughout Wisconsin and beyond the state's borders. For this reason, it seems appropriate that the "author" should be a collective one: the University of Wisconsin System Women's Studies Consortium, the organization of women's studies programs and departments throughout the University of Wisconsin System, including Extension. As the book itself makes clear, the Consortium manifests the cooperation and mutual support that has built and sustained women's studies, not only within Wisconsin, but around the U.S.

Still, because that collective author represents the work of many individuals, it is important that they also be acknowledged by name. Much of the original research for the book was done by Ellen D. Langill. This project would have been impossible to accomplish without the cooperation of the dozens of people who agreed to be interviewed, were willing to be consulted about specific details and resource materials, and added the anecdotes that appear as sidebars throughout those chapters. Their contributions are identified in the text and endnotes.

Women throughout Wisconsin, and even some who have left the state, read the sections dealing with their own campus histories in order to be sure that we had accurately captured often very complicated events: Helen Bannan, Nancy Bayne, Susan Burgess, Jane Ewens, Carol Fairbanks, Heidi Fencl, Susan Stanford Friedman, Donna Garr, Suzanne Griffith, Sarah Harder, Edna S. Hood, Shirley E. Johnson, Frances M. Kavenik, Sandra Krajewski, Estella Lauter, Tracy Luchetta, Jacqueline Macaulay, Karen Merritt, Star Olderman, Barbara Parsons, Janet Polansky, Joan I. Roberts, Virginia Sapiro, Ruth Schauer, Rachel Skalitsky, Ethel Sloane, Barbara Sniffen, Anne Statham, Kay Taube, Carol Vopat, Barbara Werner, Merry Weisner-Hanks, Kathryn Winz, and Nancy Worcester provided crucial assistance by reading large portions of the manuscript, and Mariamne Whatley deserves special thanks for patiently reading and rereading the entire thing.

Others provided forms of support without which this project would have been literally impossible. The key funding came from University of Wisconsin System President Katharine C. Lyall, with additional funding from David J. Ward, Senior Vice President for Academic Affairs, and Al Beaver, Interim Chancellor, UW Extension. Cate Irsfeld provided her usual cheerful clerical and organizational support; Jennifer Kitchak, Christina Stross, and Geeta Raval gave valuable research and proofreading assistance. Jo Futrell performed the delicate task of translating the whole thing into a document ready to be printed.

Finally, as the editor charged with pulling all of this together, I want to give particular thanks to the two people who helped in the most practical and the most intangible ways, and who demonstrated a generous spirit of feminist collaboration under often trying circumstances. Jacqueline Ross, Women's Studies Consortium director from 1989 to 1999, not only came up with the idea for this book in the first place and procured the funding, but also read several versions of the manuscript, offered suggestions for revision, and drew on her long experience with women's studies in Wisconsin to clarify many of the events the book describes. Phyllis Holman Weisbard, the Consortium's Women's Studies Librarian, has read nearly every draft of every chapter, spent innumerable hours in meetings and discussions about the book's progress, searched through library catalogues and archives to confirm historical details and sources, supplied information for footnotes, and, perhaps most valuable of all, listened to me vent.

Introduction

In 1860, the first women students entered the University of Wisconsin in Madison, enrolled in a short-lived teacher-training program. There were no women faculty or administrators, no women on the Board of Regents overseeing the University, and no women enrolled in any other program or department.

By the late 1990s, the world of higher education for women at Wisconsin's state university has changed almost beyond recognition: Women students now outnumber men at all but one campus (UW-Platteville) of the University of Wisconsin System, and while they comprise only about 20% of the UW's faculty, women make up nearly 55% of the students overall.[1] Two campuses—UW-Milwaukee and UW-La Crosse—have women Chancellors (the campuses' most senior administrators), and the University of Wisconsin System itself has a woman president. And, perhaps most interesting of all, students at every institution in the System can take courses, and in some cases even major, in women's studies.

In a sense, this book traces the process of that change, from the earliest arguments over women's admission to the University through their acceptance as students on equal terms with men, to the mid-20th century development of special programs for mature women students, and finally, to the development, beginning in about 1970, of the new field of women's studies. These changes may seem to have little in common beyond some connection to women's education, but they are in fact linked by an important trend: Each one is a particular historical period's version of women's centuries-old struggle to be taken seriously as participants in higher education and in the larger intellectual enterprise. That movement has changed dramatically since the 19th century, and on the surface, the fight simply to get women into the college classroom may not look a lot like the fight to get a graduate minor in women's studies through various University committees. But whether as students or teachers, administrators or staff members, activists, scholars—or, in some cases, all of those—the women described in this book have been part of the movement that has insisted on their importance as both learners and producers of knowledge.

Each of these stages has also been influenced by contemporaneous debates over women's position in society. From the University's beginnings, the question of whether women would be accepted as students or teachers occurred in a larger context of arguments about women's place. Although the vote was often the most visible focus until the passage of the suffrage amendment in 1920, this was a period of heated debate over every aspect of women's rights, and women's need for and access to education was a major part of that debate. Similarly, the post-World War II rise of outreach programming directed at mature and returning women students occurred because many skilled and educated women were becoming frustrated with their lack of occupational and intellectual outlets—the very situation that led Betty Friedan to write *The Feminine Mystique* (1963), the book often credited with sparking the contemporary or "Second Wave" women's movement. And the rise of women's studies in the late '60s was so self-consciously connected to feminism that the field itself has often been called the academic arm of the women's movement.[2]

Chapter 1 describes the experiences of women students and faculty between the founding of the University of Wisconsin in 1848 and World War II, focusing primarily on the campuses in Madison and Milwaukee, but also covering events at smaller state institutions. Chapter 2 deals with the University Extension Division, a statewide institution that underwent many permutations over time. It provided crucial outreach programs throughout Wisconsin, and was, especially in the early to mid-1960s, a crucial site for the courses, conferences, and other activities that focused new attention on women's needs, and provided the first links between the University and the larger U.S. women's movement. But the bulk of this book—Chapters 3 through 8—charts the development of women's studies throughout what became the University of Wisconsin System, from its origins in campus-based feminist activism in the late 1960s to its successful institutionalization and academic successes in the late 1990s.

That history did not take place in isolation, but was instead echoed around the U.S., as women students, faculty, staff, and members of the surrounding community became activists for fundamental improvements in women's status. The rise of women's studies as an academic field practiced by teachers and scholars and enshrined in formally institutionalized programs and departments was only one result of that activism,[3] which also led to major changes in faculty hiring practices, to grievance procedures by which women could respond to sexual harassment and discrimination, and to affirmative action and other programs designed to improve women's representation on the faculty, and in administration, governance, and other aspects of university life.

In the early years of the campus women's movements, demands for curricular and pedagogical change, affirmation action, anti-discrimination procedures, and so on were closely entwined, and indeed, for many activists, it has never been possible to disentangle them completely. But gradually, as some of these changes began to take place, efforts to institutionalize and expand women's studies as an interdisciplinary academic field of study did become separate from other demands for the improvement of women's status.

Women's studies itself arose out of feminists' recognition that both the experiences and the perspectives of women had been excluded from traditional scholarship and pedagogy.[4] Influential early texts, such as Kate Millett's *Sexual Politics*, tended to analyze the stereotypes and misrepresentations perpetuated by the nearly exclusive attention to men's point of view in mainstream literature, science, history, and academia generally. Those first studies took place in both academic and popular publications; Millett's book was essentially her doctoral dissertation, but similar ideas could be found in magazines and anthologies aimed at non-scholarly readers.

However, as the initial work of pointing out these insights and recovering "lost" women writers and historical figures progressed, and as scholars working within colleges and universities began to understand the far-reaching implications of these new ideas, women's studies began to emerge as an academic field. And it was a field with an unusual agenda: Although concerned with the discovery and recovery of information about women, and with the analysis and theorization of women's position in culture and society, the ultimate goal of women's studies was the transformation of all other academic fields through the total integration of women's experience into existing disciplines. From the beginning, the assumption has been that, if feminist critiques of traditional knowledge are taken seriously, all of the research based on those traditions will be utterly changed.

Because of this sweeping goal, and because of the new field's close ties to the feminist movement from which it arose, women's studies practitioners and supporters had to deal with both external and internal conflict. Many members of the university community (in Wisconsin and elsewhere) were firmly opposed to what they saw as a faddish, overly political intervention, while feminists themselves disagreed on some of the most basic questions about how women's studies should be set up. One of the major disputes, which continues in some form to this day, revolved around the question of whether women's studies courses should be organized into autonomous programs (which would give teachers more independence but possibly less security) or "mainstreamed" into existing departments (which might make it easier to transform existing curricula, but would also make faculty subject to control by the very people whose work they were critiquing). And while feminists might be united in their commitment to women's studies itself, they were often equally divided over such political issues as sexuality and race, topics that could as easily lead to passionate conflicts in a program meeting as in an off-campus political organization.[5]

Despite this common history, the evolution of formal women's studies programs varied from campus to campus, depending on the particular climate and experiences at any particular institution. Early feminists at UW-Platteville, for instance, faced problems stemming directly from the campus's long history as a school of mining and engineering, while UW-Milwaukee's urban character meant close ties between participants in women's studies and the members of organizations serving the city's women.

Nevertheless, as the following chapters make clear, women's studies programs around the state also shared many features. For most of them, courses in the new field preceded the official establishment of a program or department, but the creation of the first "Introduction to Women's Studies" course was often an important marker that a program had reached a new stage of consolidation and coherence. While students were often able to declare individualized undergraduate women's studies majors even in the early 1970s (through such bodies as a College of Letters and Science's Committee Interdisciplinary Major program), the approval of official undergraduate certificates, minors, and majors, and graduate-level concentrations and minors were signs of women's studies' acceptance as a serious field of study and of its practitioners as a permanent part of the university community. Joint faculty appointments, solid budget support for administrators and support staff, and even, in a few cases, the granting of tenure directly within women's studies served as additional indications of security. But these things came slowly, and the women described in this book often spent many years of their academic careers laboring as volunteers to make women's studies possible.

* * * * *

A few notes about the text: This book tells the story of women's education and the evolution of women's studies within what is now the University of Wisconsin System, and it is based on archival and other research, including oral history interviews with more than 80 people. In order to be sure that the voices of those who participated in the creation and development of women's studies are heard directly, a number of sidebars have been interspersed with the narrative, in which some of those women offer reminiscences about their experiences. The stories told throughout the book only scratch the surface of this complex history, and we hope that they will move readers to continue the research begun here. With that in mind, the endnotes to each chapter point to some of the sources we have discovered.

Finally, there are two reminders of the ways in which historical change can complicate the project of describing that very change. The University of Wisconsin has undergone major shifts in organization and identity since its 1848 founding. The most important was the creation of the University of Wisconsin System in 1971 through the merger of two previously separate state systems: the University of Wisconsin (which at the time consisted of UW-Madison, UW-Milwaukee, UW-Green Bay, and UW-Parkside, plus the two-year Centers [now Colleges]) and Wisconsin State Universities (now UW-Eau Claire, UW-La Crosse, UW-Oshkosh, UW-Platteville, UW-River Falls, UW-Stevens Point, UW-Stout, UW-Superior, and UW-Whitewater), along with the University of Wisconsin Extension.

The many changes of name and institutional purpose within those systems—and in some cases within the individual institutions themselves—make their histories confusing. (For instance, the Wisconsin State Universities began in 1857 as a system of Normal [teacher-training] Schools founded between 1866 and 1916. In 1927 they began to grant bachelors' degrees in education, under the name State Teachers Colleges. This system was then reorganized in 1951 as the Wisconsin State Colleges, becoming the Wisconsin State Universities in 1964.) In the chapters that follow, each institution is identified according to its name in the period under discussion, and individual campus histories are explained in more detail where it is particularly relevant.

Second, the names of many of the women who played important roles in this story have changed over the years, as they have married, divorced, and otherwise altered their lives. Depending on the specific context, alternate names are indicated in parenthesis, and every effort has been made to be consistent so that readers can recognize the same woman's involvement even when her name changes over time. All endnote references list interview subjects by their present names.

Notes

1. Figures come from the University of Wisconsin System Office of Policy Analysis and Research. Faculty statistics are for the 1995–96 academic year, student statistics for Fall 1997.

2. In "Feminist Bywords: Women's Studies," *NWSA Journal*, Vol. 3 #3 (Autumn 1991), Sandra Coyner cites Florence Howe's 1979 use of the phrase "the educational arm of the women's movement" (349n). In her review of the field's evolution, Catherine Stimpson notes that "For some, women's studies was feminism's academic 'arm,'" *Women's Studies in the United States, A Report to the Ford Foundation* (New York: Ford Foundation, 1986), p. 12.

3. For additional information about the origins of women's studies, and of its particular history at other universities, see (among many other sources) Mariam K. Chamberlain, *Women in Academe: Progress and Prospects* (New York: Russell Sage Foundation, 1988); Marilyn Jacoby Boxer, *When Women Ask the Questions: Creating Women's Studies in America* (Baltimore: Johns Hopkins University Press, 1998); Barbara Scott Winkler, *A Comparative History of Four Women's Studies Programs, 1970 to 1985*, Ph.D. dissertation, University of Michigan, 1992; and Kathryn L. Corbett and Kathleen Preston, *From the Catbird Seat: A History of Women's Studies at Humboldt State University, 1971–1996* (Arcata, CA: Humboldt State University Press, 1998).

4. The term "women's studies" did not become standard usage until the early 1970s. Sheila Tobias coined the phrase "female studies" to describe the new field when she published the first collection of syllabi for the courses springing up around the country; see her *Female Studies: A Collection of College Syllabi and Reading Lists*, Vol. I (Pittsburgh: KNOW, Inc., 1970); and Florence Howe, *Female Studies II* (Pittsburgh: KNOW, Inc., n.d.).

5. These conflicts have been an intrinsic part of women's studies since its beginnings. One particularly important result has been the development of critiques of the field's assumptions by women of color, who have often felt excluded by work that seems to be based primarily on the experience of white, often middle-class women. In the early 1980s, a number of books appeared that began to force women's studies to reexamine its premises, some of the most influential being Gloria Hull, Barbara Smith, and Patricia Bell Scott (eds.), *But Some of Us Are Brave: Black Women's Studies* (New York: Feminist Press, 1981); Cherríe Moraga and Gloria Anzaldúa (eds.), *This Bridge Called My Back: Writing by Radical Women of Color* (Watertown, MA: Persephone Press, 1982); and Barbara Smith (ed.), *Home Girls: A Black Feminist Anthology* (New York: Kitchen Table, 1983).

Chapter 1

Women in the First Century

The fortunes of the University of Wisconsin and the struggle for women's rights have in many ways had parallel histories. Wisconsin became a state in 1848, the same year that witnessed the first Women's Rights Convention in Seneca Falls, New York, where demands for women's suffrage and equality of opportunity were first made in a major public forum. On July 26 of that year, the new state chartered a public university, to be located at the state capital of Madison. As the movement for women's emancipation spread across the country and Wisconsin, too, granted new rights to women, the University grew, but efforts to expand women's opportunities for higher education advanced only slowly.[1]

The University's founders debated the idea of opening the doors to women, and as early as 1850, the Board of Regents—the University's governing body—considered a proposal for an all-female normal (teacher-training) department, but never acted upon it. In 1854, a bill in the state legislature proposed that "the University shall be equally open to the admission of pupils of both sexes over the age of sixteen,"[2] and in 1857 the Board of Regents acknowledged the "wishes of those parents who desire University culture for their daughters."[3] But the University remained a male-only bastion until 1860, despite the growing sentiment that "God-fearing women would diminish the non-religious tone of the Godless university."[4]

The first women entered the University campus with the creation of a normal department to train teachers for the many public schools across Wisconsin, whose direct practical connection to citizens' lives would, the Regents hoped, lead to state support for the University. In 1860, 30 women and 29 men were admitted to this new department for a ten-week course of lectures, but the experimental program was suspended after its first term and did not resume until the Civil War began to drain young men away from university classrooms. After the war started in April 1861, the debate over women's access to the University was renewed, and the shortage of students, rather than a change of sentiment, was the key factor in the decision to admit women students to the University. A full normal department was opened for the 1862–63 school year, and by the following year, the department had enrolled 112 students, 76 of whom were women.[5]

Not all members of the university community were happy about this development. As one male student described it, the women came like an "army with banners, conquering and to conquer . . . with bewitching curls, and dimpled cheeks, and flowing robes, and all the panoply of feminine adornment. Worst of all, they came to stay."[6] Yet, while they appeared to the few male students left on

campus as an "onslaught," the women were not fully equal to their male counterparts. An invitation to attend any University class—a development which alarmed
some of the professors—was made out of expediency rather than principle,
because it served to keep the University's doors open in the face of decreasing
male enrollments. As one female student, Ellen Chynoweth Lyon, noted
poignantly, the normal department (located on the lower floor of what is now
Bascom Hall) "resembled a graded school in its content . . . . It is regrettable to
admit that in the early years the presence of women was rather a matter of necessity than of choice and justice, for the Civil War had so depleted the student ranks
that the University was in danger of having 'finis' prematurely written in its career
on account of the small registration."[7]

By the 1864–65 school year, 60 women and 42 men were enrolled in regular
college classes, with three women even being allowed to read Livy with the professor of classics. Some professors still opposed letting women take courses other
than in the normal department, arguing that their presence would lower the "standard of culture,"[8] but the department itself was abolished after only two years, and
with the Civil War over, the Wisconsin state legislature acted to end the debate,
decreeing in 1866 that all University departments be opened to women.

* * * *

As with many gains in women's equality, the 1866 law was compromised by excep-
tions. Paul Chadbourne, who was about to become the University's new President,
believed that other schools had found coeducation to be a failure and detrimental to
the schools' reputations, and would bring "an incalculable mischief . . . into the
institution."[9] In 1867, he persuaded the legislature to qualify its full-acceptance policy by stipulating that women's admission could be carried out with any "regulations and restrictions" determined by the Board of Regents. Following the passage
of this new law and Chadbourne's appointment as President, a separate institution
for women was chartered: the Female College, which would have its own building
and completely separate classes.

This new policy was clearly an example of "separate but unequal" education,
since the course of study for the students in the Female College was considerably
watered down from that for male students in the regular University. Higher mathematics, Greek, and Latin were eliminated, and the emphasis was put on music and
the fine arts, traditional areas of study for women. When women students enrolled
in regular University classes, they were taught in separate rooms at separate times
by the same professor (thus doubling the faculty workload) and had to recite mem-
orized lessons and take examinations separately.[10]

The Female College was extremely unpopular among women students, and
one of them, Jennie Field Bashford, was so irritated by its low standards that she

wrote: "In those days the old notion of women's inferiority to man had not yet been exploded and the feminine mind was kept in a constant state of irritation by the subordinate position assigned to it at the University."[11] Although many women, like Bashford, chafed under the inferior treatment and the restrictive rules accorded them, though, the first six graduates of the Female College received the same University "bachelor's" degrees as their male counterparts in 1869. However, the University's first women graduates were almost denied this distinction, for Chadbourne stated vociferously, "Never will I be guilty of the absurdity of calling young women bachelors." Research in Webster's Dictionary paid off, since "bachelor" was also defined as an "unmarried woman," and Chadbourne had to yield.[12]

Chadbourne soon left the University, the Female College was closed, and men and women students began to attend the same classes again, even taking exams at the same time. In 1871, President John Twombly brought a more enlightened view, writing that more than thirty college presidents from across the country had testified that women students were capable of intellectually rigorous college courses.[13] Instead of spending money for separate classes, the state allotted $50,000 to build the first women's dormitory, later ironically named "Chadbourne Hall."[14] A champion of coeducation, Twombly "emphasized the inalienable right of every individual to full equality of cultural opportunity,"[15] but he could not completely conquer the residue of resentment among some male students and faculty that women were interlopers, invading the all-male bastion of the regular University classes.

The University's Board of Visitors—a citizen group with oversight powers—seconded Twombly's new approach to women's education, firmly stating their belief that "woman possesses a rational soul, and in this very fact she has a Divine warrant for the exercise and improvement of her powers . . . Her development should be limited only by her capacities and opportunities."[16] Even though some recitations continued to be conducted separately, the 1874 graduation was the last one in which men and women received diplomas at separate ceremonies. That class consisted of 26 male and 16 female students, but the women outnumbered the men on the stage when academic honors were recognized and one, Jennie Field, captured every top honor from the College of Arts. One campus publication declared: "Soon we shall see the 'Amazonian Brigade' present arms and right-shoulder shift at the voice of command."[17]

Despite the seeming victory over prejudice that this ceremony represented, it disguised the fact that women students still felt that many professors were unwilling to treat them as equals. There even appeared to be a concerted effort on the part of some faculty members to enroll as many men and as few women as possible in their courses and to deny women academic honors, as though it were a professional embarrassment to the professors.

* * * * *

1884 was also the year that John Bascom, a staunch believer in equality for women, became the University's President. Bascom and his wife Emma—an activist in the women's movement—arrived in Madison with the full conviction that women were equal in mental abilities to their male counterparts and should be accorded equal access to higher learning.

Yet even Bascom had to fight a continuing rear-guard action coming from more conservative members of the Board of Visitors, who raised the new specter that mental exertion could harm women physically. Couched in the rhetoric of preserving women's health, the Visitors espoused a conventional position of the period, cautioning that women students were jeopardizing their physical well-being by taking the vigorous course of regular University studies. Witnessing the examinations in 1877, the Visitors commented on the sickly appearance of the women students. Dismissing Bascom's argument that stress took a toll on both genders at examination time, they emphasized the particular physiology of women, wherein "nature, at stated times, makes a great demand upon the energies." "Overwork," they argued, "manifests itself by bloodlessness . . . sallow features, lack of color and . . . an absolute expression of anaemia," and proposed that less be demanded from women students in order to keep the state's future mothers "robust and hearty."[18] (Bascom was not alone among reformers in wondering why the Visitors were so concerned about the health of women students at the University when few people seemed concerned about the rigors required of women teachers or factory workers.[19])

One hundred years later, new courses in women's physiology would provide the opportunity to study the issue of stress more carefully. However, in the 1870s, a belief in the "frailties of womanhood" was part of American culture. Fortunately, the Regents rejected the proposal to water down the curriculum for women students and to once again establish a separate Female College. Instead, they lengthened the potential time to gain a degree to six years for any student whose health precluded more intensive study.

Coeducation was generally accepted by this time, as women became more vocal and more visible in many areas of public life, not the least of which was in the crusade for fuller social and political equality. University leaders like Bascom endorsed the suffrage movement, which had been an important issue for many women affiliated with the University since the founding of the Wisconsin Woman Suffrage Association (WWSA). Clara Bewick Colby, for example—one of the University's first women graduates—later became a leader in the national suffrage campaign, and many Madison women, like the President's wife Emma Bascom, were active in the WWSA, working with university graduates across the country who pushed for suffrage.[20]

John Bascom had long articulated the responsibility of educated citizens, and of the University itself, to take an active role in public service. Many scholars attribute the core of the movement that would become known as the "Wisconsin Idea" to Bascom's teachings, which emphasized the sacred duty of the University to bring about the realization of the "Christian State," part of the activist crusade that came to be known as the Social Gospel in the late nineteenth century. Involving University women in this important social crusade was a natural step for Bascom, partly because his wife was also an activist in so many reform causes of the day.[21] (Emma Bascom later became simultaneously the leader of both the Wisconsin Woman Suffrage Association and the Women's Christian Temperance Union, championing causes such as "equal pay for equal work," membership of women on juries, hiring female officers in prisons, as well as temperance and suffrage.) The Bascoms' activism and inspiring leadership of University students, both male and female, helped to set the stage for the later idealism of the Wisconsin Idea.[22]

* * * * *

Despite these successes, there were ongoing discussions between Visitors and Regents about the degree of women's inclusion in campus life. Initially, many who accepted the idea of coeducation did so in the name of "civilizing" male students with the presence of females. One professor had noted in 1864 that his women students "were certainly not inferior to the young men, while their presence evidently exerted a beneficial influence on the deportment of the latter."[23] (Others defended women's influence on less elevated grounds by noting that when their beauty was present in a classroom the attendance record of the male students improved dramatically.)

However, by the 1890s, after almost three decades of coeducation at the University, the arguments became less focused on women as moral guardians and more clearly centered on women's intellectual abilities. In an 1892 issue of the new student newspaper, the *Daily Cardinal*, the editor defended coeducation by arguing that having women in classrooms "certainly stimulates a healthy rivalry and gives young men a broader view on the ability of women to care for themselves."[24]

In 1907, University President Charles Van Hise stumbled when he proposed a separate course for women students in political economy. The original idea had actually been advanced by Professor Richard Ely, who wanted to attract more women students into his courses and believed that such a separate course might be the way to do so. However, the storm of protest from alumnae revealed just how powerful the voices of some female University graduates had become. Helen Remington Olin (Class of 1875) published a pamphlet in opposition to the move and Wisconsin Governor Robert LaFollette and his wife Belle Case LaFollette, both students in the Bascom era (Belle was the first woman to graduate from the University of Wisconsin Law School), also registered a protest, writing that they "should regret to see the University of Wisconsin take any step that might directly or indirectly be construed as a recognition for the principle of segregation."[25]

The controversy proved to be fruitful: Not only did the Regents turn down the idea of a separate course, but the legislature decided to revoke the 1867 clause permitting "regulations and restrictions upon coeducation" at the University. The replacement clause asserted that "all schools and colleges of the University shall, in their respective departments and class exercises, be open without distinction to students of both sexes." Olin celebrated with the publication of her own book on the "Women of a State University."[26] A follow-up article in *Harper's Weekly* dealing with the Van Hise controversy viewed Wisconsin as a continuous testing ground for the true value of coeducation, "whether it is the best way, or even a good way, to bring out the finest qualities and powers of a woman's soul."[27]

Still, this victory, like all others, masked the still discriminatory nature of life on campus for women students. While they could enroll in courses across the entire curriculum, they were still steered toward specific majors and urged to avoid others. English, languages, and the humanities were popular majors, with the sciences, engineering, and mathematics drawing only a rare few women into classrooms.

At the same time that students in Madison were struggling over coeducation at the University, the Wisconsin state legislature decided to expand the offerings of higher education beyond the capital, chartering several state normal schools in Platteville (1866), Whitewater (1868), Oshkosh (1871), River Falls (1873), and Milwaukee (1880).[28] Attended mostly by women students, these schools prepared teachers for the state's public schools, and although they did not grant bachelor's degrees or necessarily provide credits that allowed students to transfer to the University, they greatly increased the number of educated women in Wisconsin. In fact, one historian has argued that since teachers actually did not need a formal degree to teach public school in Wisconsin, many of the students at these normal schools were there as much for the college education as for the vocational training or teaching credentials.[29]

Other new female-dominated courses of study were also developing in this era, such as library science. University of Wisconsin courses for library workers had been offered during the 1895 summer session, and in 1906, a full-fledged library school became part of the University. Between 1895 and 1939, more than 96% of the students in the library curriculum were women.[30] In contrast, the School of Mining, located in Platteville, had only a handful of women students enrolled between 1896 and 1899, and the University's School of Medicine (established in 1907) had only three women in its first class of 26 graduates. The University Law School, too, enrolled a total of only 16 women between 1875 and 1919, while in a more traditional "women's" field, the School of Music (established in 1909) had more than three times that number.[31] The School of Music also became a larger employer of women faculty than any University program outside of home economics. This fact was significant because employment for women in the male-dominated fields of engineering and law was very difficult, thus lowering the incentive for entering those programs. In some cases, legal barriers—such as Chief Justice Edmund Ryan's dictum in 1875 denying Wisconsin women admission to the state bar—exacerbated the situation.[32]

* * * * *

It was during the great decades of progressive reform and the renewed women's rights campaign of the early twentieth century that the voices of women students were heard more powerfully on campus and within the arena of state politics. Aroused by the continuing battle over their status at the University, women students looked to other fronts to test their equality as members of the university community. They found that in the area of extracurricular activities, they had not achieved any measure of equal opportunity in their four decades as University students. At the forefront were issues such as membership in student groups, clubs, and athletics. A new battle began as women struggled to become fully part of the University as participants, not just as onlookers, in campus activities and events.[33]

Separation of social activities had begun when the first literary circle for women students, the Castalian, was organized by acting President John Sterling's wife at their home near the campus in 1864. The original plan for the University's normal department had promised women students that they would have their own gym, club room, and a program for gymnastic exercises, but these had not materialized, and even during the earliest years under Presidents Twombly and Bascom, women students had been denied opportunities in athletics and in campus activities such as literary clubs and class-sponsored events. In 1874, women students had gained the right to use the gymnasium two days a week, but could not participate in the social or political club activities sponsored by each class. During the late 1890s, the University allowed women students to organize and compete in women's basketball, a sport that was becoming increasingly popular among both sexes, but other competitive sports were off-limits.[34]

As more fraternities and sororities were founded on campus and as more students lived in private housing rather than in dormitories (of which few existed), questions arose over the issue of regulating women's social behavior. Not content to merely supervise the women students' academic or social progress, the University's first Dean of Women, Annie Crosby Emery (1897–1903), worked to establish the Women's Self-Government Association (WSGA). This association had the power to supervise the social activities of women students (and was sometimes resented for doing so) and served as a training ground, educating women for roles in reform and politics. It also became a forum where women's voices could be heard without ridicule and where rules, athletics, and social activities could be discussed freely.[35]

The WSGA debated matters such as curfews (usually 10:30 p.m.), dormitory rules, visitation rules for gentlemen in dormitory lounges, and other matters. These matters came to a head in 1898 when a prank parade and serenade of Ladies Hall turned into an invasion. Male students broke into the hall and over $500 worth of clothing was stolen from the laundry room as "trophies of the escapade."[36] In retaliation, the women students organized for the first time as a unit and vowed to replicate the protests of their fictional Greek sisters in the Aristophanes play *Lysistrata*. They resolved to "have no social relations with the men of the University until the faculty or men of the University have satisfactorily dealt with the offenders . . . and until all losses sustained at that time have been made good."[37] The boycott, approved by a 80 to 55 vote of the women students, lasted until the perpetrators were caught and suspended. Clearly, the women students of the University had achieved the ability to unite and take action through democratic means.

Finally, in 1909, the beginnings of a social and athletic program for women students was inaugurated with the completion of Lathrop Hall, which complemented Chadbourne Hall's dormitory facilities with a new gymnasium, dance rooms, club rooms and social centers. The ideal of social service was the key theme in the dedication ceremonies for Lathrop Hall in April 1909. Speaking to the women students, Anna Garlin Spencer, of the New York School of Philanthropy, called upon Wisconsin's women students and faculty to achieve the "new feminine ideal of dignity . . . for the highest social service."[38]

Women's presence at the University now had a physical center in Lathrop Hall, which included home economics laboratories and an office for the Dean of Women. Although the Dean set the parameters, the women students' ability to govern themselves through the WSGA proved to be a stimulus to further independence. Separation from male extracurricular activities was still the norm, though. Excluded from the Student Union, the women established other clubs and literary societies, the counterparts of the men's clubs that had dominated campus social life since the beginning.

The idea of women students living, often unchaperoned, in rooming houses across the city was abhorrent to many, and the resulting demand for supervised housing was met with the establishment of cooperative housing units, where women students shared expenses or small jobs. Infractions in the coop houses, as in all campus living units, were met with University discipline, but the women students were soon granted the opportunity to adjudicate these disciplinary problems, another step forward in the on-campus training for political participation.[39]

The University's second Dean of Women, Cora S. Woodward (1907-1911), established a Woman's Court to hear cases regarding women students. Infractions included sneaking in after hours, being caught in the women's lounge with a man after hours, smoking, drinking, or even using profanity. The most common punishments were loss of privileges for several days or a week, but more serious matters could be referred to the Dean of Women for actions, including suspension or expulsion. Dressing inappropriately (one young woman substituted green hosiery for the acceptable brown color) could also bring complaints and some form of punishment. While these restrictions may seem excessive from the perspective of the 1990s, the WSGA and its court continued to hold the loyalty of the women students as positive measures in their ability to control their social roles within the university community.[40]

The enrollment of women students at the University also soared in this period. In the academic year 1909–1910, there were 1,103 women students of more than 4,000 total enrolled, and the following year, the number of women grew to 1,589. Housing was scattered across town, and caring for those who lived off campus became a central concern of the Dean of Women. The WSGA tried to link women students by providing representation from all of the living units, dormitories, and sorority houses where women students resided.[41] The Dean of Women's office also began to publish a student handbook where rules concerning curfew and social conduct for women students were clearly listed.

Lathrop Hall not only became the center for women's self-government, but served as a gathering place for all women students, since they were not permitted membership at Memorial Union on Langdon Street. "Mixers" and other social gatherings were held at Lathrop, which became the stimulus for the formation of women's class clubs.[42] The freshmen women organized their own club named the Green Buttons (analogous to the men's Green Beanie club); the sophomores became the Red Gauntlets, the juniors the Yellow Tassels, and the seniors the Blue Dragons. Out of these class clubs came greatly increased social cohesion for women students, as well as more athletic opportunities as intramural sports were organized in volleyball, tennis, bowling, swimming, and basketball. The clubs also sponsored a May Fête with a Maypole each spring prior to graduation.[43]

Excluded from the male-controlled student publications and literary societies, the women students also sponsored their own similar activities. The oldest women's literary society, the Castalian, was joined by the Pythia in 1902. Soon the Red Dominoes, for women interested in drama, was organized, along with the Girls' Glee Club, Orchesis for those interested in modern dance, and the Dolphins for swimmers. In 1917, the Outing Club for women students sponsored sailing events, canoeing, hiking and skiing trips, later imitated by the all-male Hoofers Club.[44]

In addition to these social and recreational activities, women students and their self-government association protested ongoing patterns of discrimination both inside and outside of the classroom. One student wrote that in her chemistry class, since the male students greatly outnumbered the women, the latter had to sit at the rear of the classroom and received the least attention from the professor. The few women professors at the University also fought battles on behalf of the women students, first in the area of physical education, where classes remained separate for men and women. Beginning in 1912, Blanche Trilling, Director of Women's Physical Education, petitioned the University for a women's building at Camp

Randall, since the women students had nowhere to change for field hockey, fencing, or other sports and were forbidden to walk across campus in their sports attire. A tent was pitched at the site as a changing room until 1915, when a permanent new facility was completed.[45]

Another closed door was in student publications, where the *Daily Cardinal* had been an all-male organization since its founding in 1892. A journalism professor supported the protests of women who wanted a say in the campus press, but no changes were made until World War I took many male students away from campus and women were finally included on the paper's staff. As a partial compromise beginning in 1910, women students were allowed to publish one issue of the *Cardinal*—dubbed the *Coed Cardinal*—each year, to test their ability to handle "hard news."[46]

While women undergraduates struggled to find a voice, women graduate students did not exhibit the same aspirations to belong to the social life on campus, perhaps because they were still dealing with fundamental questions about their right to pursue degrees and hold professional positions. In 1904, the University organized a graduate program, awarding its first Ph.D. degree to Charles Van Hise, who had become University President the previous year. In 1906, the Regents officially announced that the graduate school would serve the needs of "young men and women of college training who desire a larger and more thorough acquaintance with the scholarship and research of the world."[47] Graduate students, most of whom lived independently, were not included in dormitory rules or in the self-government association.

However, Van Hise had already made it clear that he would not personally encourage women to pursue graduate studies. Telling the Regents that fellowships awarded to women were not productive, Van Hise stated that although he favored coeducation on the undergraduate level, he had "reservations about graduate work for women." Arguing that "the percentage of women who are willing to work at the same subject six hours a day for three hundred days in the year is much smaller than among the men."[48]

Whether or not Van Hise's assessment of women's academic ambitions was correct, the price paid by most women who received Ph.D. degrees from American universities in this early era was to delay or even to forego marriage. A study of more than one thousand women who had received Ph.D.'s between 1877 and 1929 found that 75 percent had remained single. Most of the women students in the University of Wisconsin's graduate program were enrolled in summer courses rather than traditional full-year academic programs. Many of these women were already employed in their chosen fields—often education or library science—and entered the graduate program for career advancement, rather than to become scholars or university professors.[49]

It was University of Wisconsin Regent Zona Gale who first brought the attention of the Board to the issue of discrimination against women faculty at the University. One national study, conducted in 1927, revealed the problem of salary discrepancy between male and female teachers at universities across the country. Inspired by this research, Gale wrote to Elizabeth Waters (who had just left the Board of Regents) and included a list of faculty rankings by gender, which showed that only women in the home economics department had been able to attain full professorships.

Women interested in college and university teaching often found that obtaining the higher degree left them unemployable. The records of scholars such as historians Martha Letitia Edwards (who received her doctorate from the UW in 1916) and Florence Porter Robinson (M.A., 1892), indicate that they had to seek jobs at the country's few women's colleges or accept only untenured lectureships. Robinson actually had to change fields from history to home economics before she could find work at the university level. One graduate received a candid reply from a college where she sought employment, stating that the school "would rather have a second-rate man than a first-rate woman."[50] Discrimination against women faculty in both hiring and promotion came on the heels of their first admittance to graduate programs and was an institutional problem that not only went without solution for many more decades, but actually worsened as the century wore on.[51]

* * * * *

In addition to fighting battles for equality on campus, University of Wisconsin students were involved in causes outside the campus walls, many of them specifically of relevance to women's lives. On campus and off, they crusaded for suffrage, peace, temperance, and what were, at the time, explicitly Socialist reforms such as more playgrounds, regulation or ownership of utilities, and a stronger role for government in creating a better society.

Some of these activities were extremely controversial, raising basic issues such as the limits of free speech on campus. For example, the Social Science Club—one of the very first truly coed student organizations at the University—hoped to bring in speakers who would address great issues of the day, but ran afoul of several conservative factions on campus and on the Board of Regents and was denied the right to invite radical speakers such as Upton Sinclair.[52] Active on both sides of this question were the two women Regents mentioned above: Elizabeth Waters, who opposed allowing an open forum, and the more liberal Zona Gale, a staunch defender of academic freedom.[53] The result of this particular fight was the Board of Regents' addition to the University bylaws of the now-famous defense of academic freedom: "we believe that the Great State of Wisconsin should ever encourage that continual and fearless sifting and winnowing by which alone the truth can be found."[54]

While women on the faculty endured the hardships of few promotions and low salaries, women students became caught up in the ongoing progressive spirit of the period, as the Progressive Movement inspired many young people to become involved in social reform causes. Women at the UW, for example, established a chapter of the Intercollegiate Prohibition Society to wage a war on "demon rum"—often considered a "progressive" cause in this period. Another cause which enlisted women students was support for the Women's Trade Union League, through which collections were sent to women on strike, including the 1910 New York shirtwaist makers' strike. The *Coed Cardinal* (published annually after 1910) praised the activism of these women: "University women . . . have truly manifested their interest in the great woman movement."[55]

But "the woman movement" in these pre-World War I years meant, above all, the crusade for the vote. As the suffrage movement escalated in intensity, many women students and faculty members took an active role. Using their yearly *Daily Cardinal* issue, the women editors blared forth the headline "Votes for Women" as the Wisconsin referendum on suffrage was hotly debated.[56] A large number of alumnae were very visible in the state campaign. Florence Kelley—who later emerged as a leader in the women's labor movement and at Hull House, the Chicago settlement center—came to Madison to help in the final push. Belle Case LaFollette, whose husband was in the U.S. Senate by then, returned to Wisconsin to give 31 speeches in a twelve-day tour of the state.[57]

However, Wisconsin's liquor lobby was able to persuade many of Wisconsin's legislators that suffrage for women would mean prohibition of alcohol because of the very close association between the suffrage and temperance movements. (In fact, even at the national level, the so-called Prohibition amendment [the 18th] actually preceded the women's suffrage amendment [the 19th], which passed only after the liquor lobby had been substantially defused during the Germanophobia of World War I.)

As the drive for state-by-state passage of suffrage laws failed, the push for a national suffrage amendment—nicknamed "the Anthony Amendment" after suffrage leader Susan B. Anthony—moved forward with new vigor after 1913. Once again, many students, faculty, and alumnae of the University and the state's many normal schools took part. The UW chapter of the National American Woman Suffrage Association (NAWSA) organized an all-student effort on behalf of the Anthony Amendment and was successful in getting 97% of the University faculty to declare in favor of votes for women. By April of 1919, the Madison student suffragists were organizing weekly marches on the Capitol, demonstrating President Van Hise's description of State Street as a linkage between campus and government. Banners hung across Lathrop Hall proclaiming "Come, let's go to the Legislature!"[58] The campus branch of the WWSA held weekly meetings, and by May of 1919 its members numbered more than 300, many of whom championed suffrage because it would lead to an expanded role for women in all areas of political life. As one student suffragist, Elsa Gluck, wrote, "The University of Wisconsin is doing everything it can to prepare its women for the largest possible share in public service."[59]

Just as University classes were ending in June, 1919, Congress passed the Anthony Amendment. The Wisconsin legislature, still in session, ratified the new suffrage amendment immediately and sent its notice to Washington, just before that of Illinois.[60] Wisconsin thus became the first state to register its ratification of the 19th amendment, an achievement that brought jubilation among the ranks of the WWSA. Victory parades marched down State Street and around the Capitol Square with student suffragists joining the throng of women wearing the clothes that had come to be associated with the movement: white dresses with yellow suffrage sashes. Women at the University of Wisconsin and at normal schools from Milwaukee to Platteville had proven that their activism in social causes outside of the University's walls could bring positive results.[61]

During the second decade of the twentieth century, the number of women students and faculty at the University in Madison and at the normal schools grew substantially. Many of these women were not only dedicated scholars and teachers, but they also embraced the University's ideal of service to their communities beyond the walls of the classroom. During his tenure as University President, Charles Van Hise enunciated the concept, labeled "the Wisconsin Idea," of expanding the role of the University, making it an institution of research and a key resource to state government, and extending its metaphorical boundaries to the boundaries of the state. Van Hise's "ideal of service" grew to include many facets of university life, from the work of professors in advising the legislature on social and economic reforms, to the service by other professors to all sectors of the state's population and industry. It also came to include many women in its embrace, as programs evolved through the School of Agriculture to serve rural Wisconsin, and as Extension programs grew to provide service and education to people across the state.[62]

Progressive men and women endorsed Van Hise's ideal. The power of this link between the University and the state would be felt in government and social institutions for many decades. Even as he outlined his thoughts, Van Hise included women in the statement of his ideal university: "I shall never rest content until the beneficent influences of the university are made available to every home in the state . . . a university supported by the state for all its people, for its sons and daughters."[63]

During Van Hise's presidency, the Extension Division was established (1906), as a revival of the University Extension activities of the 1890s.[64] Short courses that served farmers across the state had been in existence for more than 20 years by then, for, like all land-grant schools, Wisconsin was mandated to provide services to farmers and others throughout the state. During the next two decades, however, the University of Wisconsin broadened these outreach efforts under the philosophy expressed by President Thomas K. Chamberlin:

> I would recommend the adoption of a broad general policy . . . and would advise that the University offer all the aid which the Faculty can give . . . to

> local organizations . . . to educate the people in any industry or calling or in
> general culture or in any useful line. I believe that the giving of such aid freely
> . . . will conduce to the great end sought by the University.[65]

Historian Frederick Jackson Turner added a metaphor of his own regarding the
pivotal role of programs like Wisconsin's: "There is in this machinery a means for
exercising a most quickening and elevating influence upon the village life of the
State, and for carrying irrigating streams of education into the arid regions of the
State."[66] With its formal organization in 1906 as a distinct program of the
University (followed in 1914 by the establishment of the Agricultural Extension
Service), Extension was poised to become the leading embodiment of the service
and outreach ideal of the Wisconsin Idea.

As it expanded, the University Extension Division (whose particular history
with regard to women is described in Chapter 2) reached out to women as well as
men, through lecture and correspondence courses. The response from the people of
Wisconsin was tremendous. In the first several years of the lecture program alone,
more than 50 courses drew in an average attendance of almost 200 people each,
leading President Chamberlin to estimate that nearly 9,000 people had been
reached by the training.

Women faculty at the UW and in the normal schools were already poised to
embrace the Wisconsin Idea. In fact, many had been assisting in government or
community work long before Van Hise crystallized the relationship in his
speeches, and one of the first groups of women to provide enlightened public service were those enrolled in the Library School. Through its demands for practical
experience and its internships, the Library School sent volunteers as well as faculty
consultants to help community libraries. They catalogued over 2,000 books for the
Madison Public Library and maintained free book drop-off stations at grocery
stores and fire stations throughout the city. Extending their service throughout the
state, the Library School students and faculty worked through the Free Library
Commission to assist over fifty public libraries, college libraries, and even the
inmates' library at the state prison at Waupun. This activist spirit of involvement
outside of classrooms continued after World War I. In 1922 alone, women students
at the Library School reported that 48 of its students had given more than 96
months of service to communities across Wisconsin.[67]

Some female-dominated professions actually made public service their primary focus. The School of Social Work, for instance, was founded in 1920 by
Helen Clarke, who left a job with the Red Cross in Chicago to offer the first
courses at the University. She created field placements at settlement houses, influenced by her early work under Lillian Wald at Henry Street House in New York.
During the 1920s, Clarke served on the LaFollette Committee, which established a
plan for welfare and family support in Wisconsin.[68]

* * * * *

Throughout the Van Hise years and the period of the First World War, the position of women on campus improved substantially. However, these improvements came at a price, and during the years after the suffrage victory and the war, there was a measure of backlash on campus against the many new inroads made by women students into the central halls of power.

During WWI, women students had not only entered fully into the life of the University, but had also led many war bond drives, organized a War Work Council under the leadership of the WSGA, and rolled Red Cross bandages. They had made other sacrifices as well, supporting measures to conserve food and fuel that resulted in the limitation of athletic activities and the closing of Lathrop Hall during the coldest winter months.[69] Women also had opportunities to expand their campus activities. In 1919, for example, a woman served as editor of the *Wisconsin Yearbook*, and others became a permanent part of the newspaper staff of the *Cardinal*. They also fought for and succeeded in obtaining admission to (and later full membership in) the newly-constructed Memorial Union on Langdon Street, which soon housed the offices of both the campus YWCA and the WSGA.[70]

The backlash erupted with the return to campus of soldiers, who found that things had changed dramatically. Disappointed male students created a "Society for the Welfare of Male Students" and the *Cardinal* ran a scare headline: "College Man a Mere Relic in a Few Years . . . Women are Fast Overrunning the University!" One writer put it bluntly: "The place of the Coed . . . ought to revert . . . the University ought to be just for men . . . now that the war is over."[71] Similar sentiments would echo in the years immediately following World War II.

But women students—who numbered more than 3,000 by 1920—had no intention of giving up their improved status. Louise Nardin, Dean of Women, spurred them forward, holding career seminars to interest women students in a greater variety of new fields. Twelve students in the Department of Agriculture organized the first Women's Agriculture Society in the country, and women medical students established the Medics Club. By 1921, other non-traditional majors were enrolling more women students: 179 in commerce, 112 in journalism, 24 in chemistry, 15 in medicine, 11 in pharmacy, and two in law. By 1929, there were six honorary societies which recognized women's academic achievements in diverse fields.[72]

* * * * *

The accomplishments of women faculty also helped to earn the University of Wisconsin a national reputation for innovation and academic excellence, and several of them made lasting impressions on their students and colleagues.

Helen C. White, for example, came to Madison as an English instructor in 1919 and retired in 1965—having become, in 1936, the first woman full professor in the College of Letters and Science. Her women students revered her,[73] her reputation as a influential scholar and teacher was widespread, and she received more than 20 honorary degrees during her academic career. And yet, wrote White (after whom the building that houses the English Department was eventually named), "I'm not yet dead sure that being a woman is a bad job if you have patience enough to give your days and nights to getting to be a better scholar than the men."[74]

Another member of the English faculty, Ruth Wallerstein, could become "very fierce" when she perceived that women faculty were being slighted.[75] In one notable incident, women faculty (who had finally been allowed a lounge of their own at the University Club on State Street) noticed that the magazines placed in their room by staff members included only *Harper's Bazaar* and *Vogue*. Demanding that they be allowed their own issue of the *New York Times*, Wallerstein pointed out that the male faculty lounge had a wide array of newspapers and journals available, which the women could not use, since they could not enter the male-only lounge. However, when her demand was refused by the ruling Board of the club, Wallerstein resigned in protest.[76]

Elizabeth Brandeis, a member of the economics department from 1924 to 1962, gave students a clear sense of how their government operated, through an innovative pedagogical technique. In addition to holding mock hearings on federal bills, as she recalled many years later, "I worked out a method of giving the students participation in what was happening in the state Legislature. Each student had a bill in the field of labor or social security which he or she followed: attended the hearings on it, reported the hearings in class, and wrote a brief report at the end of the semester on . . . how it would change the statute if it passed."[77] Despite her excellence as a teacher and scholar, however, Brandeis recognized that she was "certainly discriminated against on the basis of pay. If I compared myself, double my salary was less than the salary of most of my colleagues."[78] And this disparity did not only exist in her pay, but in her rank as well: She spent her entire teaching career in the position of lecturer, although she was eventually given a departmental rank of associate and then full professor, allowing her to participate in Executive Committee meetings and decision-making.[79]

Women faculty members played important roles in developing innovative programs in the arts as well. In 1926, the Regents recognized the advances made by Margaret H'Doubler in the field of modern dance, granting her the power to create the first dance major at any university in the nation, a program that gave Wisconsin prominence for many decades.[80] The development of an art program in the University also owed a great deal to a woman faculty member, Helen Annen, who also came to the University in 1926. The art program, sixteen years old at the time, had mostly included courses to supplement the program for teachers. However, it soon developed its own integrity with specialists such as Della Wilson in sculpture, and other faculty in areas such as drawing and painting, industrial arts, and design.[81]

Still, the most popular major for women students was home economics, with its faculty of 28 women, many laboratories, and a separate model cottage and farm house. Created as a University major in 1903, the home economics department grew directly out of statewide offerings through the Farm Institutes and Cooking Schools. Led by Abby L. Marlatt after 1909, the program became part of the College of Agriculture and moved into its own new Home Economics Extension Building in 1914.

The success of Marlatt's program was due in large part to her zealous commitment and to her keen understanding of politics. When her enrollment exceeded that of the entire agricultural school, she demanded better teaching facilities and increased classroom and laboratory space. Denied this by the University, she succeeded in gathering a lobby of alumnae and clubwomen from around the state, who petitioned the legislature to build a new wing onto the Extension Building. By 1925, the Department of Home Economics enrolled more than 300 full-time students, as well as many from the College of Letters and Science who took one or more courses there.

Marlatt also lobbied for and received funding and space to open a nursery school on campus in 1930, which provided practical training in both education and early childhood development and nutrition. Marlatt also remained strongly devoted to Extension programming, and for many years, she traveled the state offering courses on nutrition, home management, sanitation, and food preservation. Her strength and commitment to the women in her program became a model which many other faculty women began to emulate.[82]

* * * * *

During this same period, new public colleges and universities opened around the state, and existing ones were reorganized to serve the changing needs of Wisconsin's students.[83] The activities of women at these institutions were in many ways as influential as those in Madison. Women faculty at the Normal School at Stevens Point presided over the creation of the school's first home economics program in 1913. One professor, Bessie May Allen, created and led the Wisconsin Home Economics Association for several years, and served as president of the College Faculty. At the Stout Institute—still a private institution at the time[84]—the new manual training classes (later called industrial arts), created in 1909, were open to both women and men, the first of their kind in the country.

However, the entry of women was an uphill battle at first, as professors told them they didn't want them around machinery and slotted them instead into cooking classes. A few courageous and progressive women students finally broke down the barrier, but the first woman graduate discovered that State Senator Stout—after whom the campus was named—handed her the wrong diploma at her ceremony in 1909, completely incredulous that a woman had survived the industrial program.[85]

At the new Eau Claire Normal School in 1916, the faculty taught 141 women and 18 men students. Members of the Education Department there organized a laboratory school and several women faculty members drove across the northwest corner of the state to make sure that students who might qualify for the laboratory school would be able to attend.[86]

In Milwaukee, faculty opened a special Extension Day School in 1920 to serve veterans of WWI. During the war, faculty had participated in a program to train women to be radio electronic technicians for the military. Other women entered the civilian flight training program, receiving private pilot licenses under the auspices of the Civilian Aeronautics Authority. Soon thereafter, the school was also opened to women who could earn up to two years of university credit, but with flexible hours and scheduling. Soon the number of women enrolled outnumbered men and many students from immigrant families joined the program as well.[87]

Faculty at the Normal School in La Crosse, the first institution in Wisconsin authorized to award a diploma to women in physical education, made it their mission to work with YWCAs and Red Cross agencies across the state to help design workable recreational programs. They also pushed for the passage of a state law that mandated physical education for students in elementary schools as a way to improve the fitness of the state's youth. In 1926, faculty member Emma Lou Wilder served as president of the state's Physical Education Association and promoted the cause of competitive sports for women, creating her own tennis, basketball, and field hockey teams as models.[88]

* * * * *

As the agricultural depression swept Wisconsin in the 1920s, many students from rural areas were almost without any funds for living expenses once they paid tuition, and college and university administrators often came up with innovative solutions to assist their students. In the 1920s, Dean of Women Louise Nardin worked to set up more cooperative housing units where students could earn room and board by working, and Dean Louise Troxell (later Greeley) provided similar support during the Depression of the 1930s. A Women's Self-Employment Bureau on the University of Wisconsin campus also helped to place students in jobs to earn enough extra money to survive.

In 1933, Dean Troxell also established the Dean of Women's Fund, which she used to grant emergency loans to students, totaling more than $1,000 each year. Troxell's fund, which she raised through solicitations to businesses and alumnae, was so successful in helping women students survive the Depression that the

Dean of Men's office asked that she relinquish control to a general fund to be used for all students. Troxell angrily responded, "Money given to the Dean of Women can be spent [only] by her as Dean of Women."[89]

Although tuition for in-state students was only $27.50 per semester, living costs were ten times that much. To ease the dormitory crisis at Madison, two new facilities, Anne Emery Hall and Elizabeth Waters Hall, were constructed before the end of the 1930s. The Dean's office also helped women find part-time jobs, but reported that a crisis still existed for some students who appeared "near starvation." Enrollments remained fairly constant in the Depression years, at around 3,000, because many young people came to the University from families who could not find jobs for them or feed them at home, whereas the Dean's office could supply funds from a New Deal program, the National Youth Administration (NYA), to provide campus employment. (Such efforts weren't limited to Madison, either: At the state college at Eau Claire, Dean of Women Laura Sutherland helped students who struggled to pay tuition by organizing a fund and later using money from NYA to tide students over through campus jobs.[90]) One-fourth of the 264 women graduate students enrolled at Madison in 1937 and one-third of the women undergraduates worked at least part-time, and many were completely self-supporting.

The voices of women on campus throughout the 1930s continued to command respect, both in their own separate student organizations and in the campus-wide forums which were open to them. By the end of the decade, the Women's Self-Government Association (WSGA) was joined in campus governance by the coeducational Union Council, later known as the Wisconsin Student Association, and in 1939, for the first time, a woman was elected president of the senior class.[91]

As the 1930s ended, the 3,269 women students on the Madison campus watched as the world was once again plunged into war with Hitler's invasion of Poland in September, 1939. Dean Troxell described how the University had prepared women to face whatever challenges the war might bring: "Women in our university are strategically situated . . . to work, both socially and politically . . . with men . . . The threats of war make it important that we have and disseminate all possible information about new work for women and also the ramifications of the defense program for our women students."[92]

Notes

1. 1833 marked the establishment of Oberlin College, the first in the U.S. to admit women on the same terms as men; Mt. Holyoke, the first college for women, was founded in 1837. The University of Iowa, established in 1855, was the first state university to admit women from its opening days.

2. Quoted in Merle Curti and Vernon Carstensen, *The University of Wisconsin, A History, 1848–1925* (Madison: University of Wisconsin Press, 1949), Vol. I, p. 101.

3. Quoted in Jean Droste, "Coeducation 1849–1909: They Came to Stay," in Marian J. Swoboda and Audrey J. Roberts (eds.), *They Came to Teach, They Came to Learn, They Came to Stay*, University Women: A Series of Essays (Madison: University of Wisconsin System Office of Women, 1980), Vol. I, p. 2.

4. Curti and Carstensen, Vol. I, pp. 24, 101; Droste, "Coeducation 1849–1909," pp. 1, 2.

5. Droste, "Coeducation 1849–1909," p. 3.

6. Droste, "Coeducation 1849–1909," p. 3.

7. Quoted in Droste, "Coeducation 1849–1909," p. 3.

8. Curti and Carstensen, Vol. I, p. 119.

9. Quoted in Droste, "Coeducation 1849–1909," p. 3.

10. Curti and Carstensen, Vol. I, p. 371.

11. Quoted in Droste, "Coeducation 1849–1909," p. 4.

12. Curti and Carstensen, Vol. I, pp. 371–372.

13. Droste, "Coeducation 1849–1909," p. 4.

14. Edward Birge, University President when the building was named, later said that he "thought it only fair that Dr. Chadbourne's contumacy regarding coeducation should be punished by attaching [his name] to a building which turned out [to be] one of the main supports of coeducation." Quoted in Ellen D. Langill, "Women at Wisconsin: 1909–1939," in Swoboda and Roberts, Vol. I, p. 12.

15. Curti and Carstensen, Vol. I, p. 373.

16. Quoted in Droste, "Coeducation 1849–1909," p. 5.

17. Curti and Carstensen, Vol. I, p. 374.

18. Curti and Carstensen, Vol. I, p. 377..

19. Droste, "Coeducation 1849–1909," pp. 5–6.

20. Genevieve G. McBride, *On Wisconsin Women: Working for Their Rights from Settlement to Suffrage* (Madison: University of Wisconsin Press, 1993), pp. 291–293.

21. Curti and Carstensen, Vol. I, p. 287.

22. McBride, p. 112. The Bascoms' youngest child, Florence (1862–1945), became

the first woman geologist in the U.S., was only the second woman to earn a doctorate in the field (Johns Hopkins University, 1893), and founded the geology department at Bryn Mawr College. She also received undergraduate and graduate degrees from the University of Wisconsin (Bachelor's degree in Arts & Letters, 1882; Bachelor's degree in Science, 1884; M.A., 1887). A capsule biography is available online at <http://geoclio.st.usm.edu/fbascom.html>; see also Isabel Fothergill Smith, *The Stone Lady: A Memoir of Florence Bascom* (Bryn Mawr, PA: Bryn Mawr College, 1981).

23. Quoted in Curti and Carstensen, Vol. I, p. 118.

24. Quoted in Droste, "Coeducation 1849–1909," pp. 6–7.

25. Droste, "Coeducation 1849–1909," p. 7; Helen Remington Olin, *The Women of a State University* (New York: G.P. Putnam's Sons, 1909).

26. Droste, "Coeducation 1849–1909," p. 7.

27. Quoted in Langill, p. 11.

28. Richard N. Current, *The History of Wisconsin, The Civil War Era, 1848–1873,* Volume II (Madison: The State Historical Society of Wisconsin, 1976), p. 508.

29. Current, p. 508.

30. Valmai Fenster, "Women's Contributions to the Library School: 1895–1939," in Marian Swoboda and Audrey Roberts (eds.), *Wisconsin Women, Graduate School, and the Professions*, University Women: A Series of Essays (Madison: University of Wisconsin System Office of Women, 1980), Vol. II, p. 21.

31. Lois Greenfield, "Women in Engineering: Highlights and Shadows," in Swoboda and Roberts, Vol. II, pp. 29–39; Rima D. Apple and Judith Walzer Leavitt, "Women in Medical School," in Swoboda and Roberts, Vol. II, pp. 55–64.

32. Ruth B. Doyle, "Women and the Law School, From a Trickle to a Flood," in Swoboda and Roberts, Vol. II, pp. 65–73; Carolyn Sylvander, "Women in the School of Music," in Swoboda and Roberts, Vol. II, pp. 75–78; Catherine B. Cleary, "Lavinia Goodell, First Woman Lawyer in Wisconsin," *Wisconsin Magazine of History*, Vol. 74, Summer 1991.

33. Langill, pp. 11–12.

34. Langill, pp. 12–13; Curti and Carstensen, Vol. I, p. 375.

35. Langill, p. 13; Curti and Carstensen, Vol. I, p. 669.

36. Curti and Carstensen, Vol. I, p. 675.

37. Quoted in Curti and Carstensen, Vol. I, p. 675.

38. Langill, p. 12.

39. Langill, p. 12.

40. Langill, p. 12.

41. Langill, p. 12.

42. Langill, pp. 13–14.

43. Langill, pp. 13–14.

44. Langill, pp. 13–14.

45. Langill, pp. 13–14. This exclusion from athletic facilities continued to be contentious six decades later, when women students and faculty once again protested their second-class facilities; see Chapter 4.

46. Langill, p. 17.

47. Jean Droste, "Vocational Aspirations and Job Realities: A Look at Some Women Receiving Ph.D.'s prior to 1926," in Swoboda and Roberts, Vol. II, pp. 1–3.

48. Droste, "Vocational Aspirations and Job Realities," pp. 1–3.

49. Droste, "Vocational Aspirations and Job Realities," pp. 1–3.

50. Droste, "Vocational Aspirations and Job Realities," pp. 5–7.

51. Droste, "Vocational Aspirations and Job Realities," p. 7.

52. Langill, p. 18; Curti and Carstensen, Vol. II, pp. 155–157.

53. From the founding of the University of Wisconsin through 1971, when the University of Wisconsin System was created, only fourteen women served as members of the Board of Regents. They were: **Miss Almah Frisby** (served 1901–6), Milwaukee, physician and professor of hygiene and sanitary science; **Florence Buckstaff** (1907–23), B.A. (1886) and M.A. from University of Wisconsin, thesis on "Married Women's Property Rights in Anglo-Saxon and Anglo-Norman Law"; **Mrs. E. Ray Stevens (Kate L. Sabin Stevens)** (1906–7), Madison, Dane County Superintendent of Schools prior to her marriage; **Miss Elizabeth Waters** (1911–15, 1921–33), Fond du Lac, taught English, mathematics and German in Fond du Lac schools and became principal (in 38 years of teaching, she was never absent a single day due to sickness; UW-Madison dormitory bears her name); **Miss Frances Perkins** (1915–21), Fond du Lac, teacher, social worker, and American Association of University Women activist; **Miss Leola Hirschman** (1922–28), Milwaukee, long-time secretary to Milwaukee lawyer and author William B. Rubin, affiliated with many clubs, including National Council of Jewish Women; **Miss Zona Gale** (1923–29), Portage, Pulitzer-prize-winning author, Progressive Party activist, chair of Wisconsin Free Library Commission, donator of scholarships in her name; **Mrs. Clara T. Runge** (1926–38), Baraboo, active in organizations, treasurer of Wisconsin Foundation of Women's Clubs (1918), member of Board of Regents of the Normal Schools before appointment to University Board of Regents; **Mrs. Meta Berger** (1928–34), Milwaukee, 19-year member of Milwaukee School Board, member of Board of Regents of the Teachers' Colleges, wife of socialist Victor Berger; **Mrs. Jesse C. Combs** (1933–39), Oshkosh, librarian prior to her marriage, member of Twentieth Century Club, Board of Directors of Oshkosh Community Chest; **Mrs. John Campbell (Mary)** (1938–39), Dodgeville, a nurse prior to her marriage, prominent in Progressive Party activity, State Chair of Women's Division (1936); **Mrs. Barbara Vergeront** (1939–43), Viroqua, teacher prior to her marriage, operated

farm with her husband, leader in Republican women's groups, member of Statewide Committee on the Centenary of the University (1948); **Helen C. Laird** (1951–59), Marshfield, secretary of the family business, served on many community boards, delegate to 1950 Republican convention, mother of Congressman and Secretary of Defense Melvin Laird, Jr.; **Caroline T. Sandin** (1968–71), Ashland, teacher prior to her marriage, active in Ashland League of Women Voters and president of Tri-County Medical Society Auxiliary. This list uses the form of name provided in *The Board of Regents of the University of Wisconsin During the Years 1849–1971*, a loose-leaf collection of brief biographies (University Archives).

54. Quoted in Curti and Carstensen, Vol. II, p.155.

55. Langill, pp. 16–18; McBride, pp. 207–210.

56. Langill, pp. 16–18; McBride, pp. 207–210.

57. McBride, pp. 208–209.

58. Langill, p. 21.

59. Langill, p. 21.

60. In fact, Illinois passed the Amendment first, but because of a procedural error that could not be corrected in time, Wisconsin became the first state officially to ratify it; Genevieve G. McBride, *On Wisconsin Women*, pp. 290–291.

61. Langill, pp. 21–23.

62. Curti and Carstensen, Vol. II, p. 586.

63. Quoted in Langill, p.12.

64. Personal communication, Shirley E. Johnson to Jacqueline Ross, March 19, 1999.

65. Quoted in Curti and Carstensen, Vol. I, p. 715.

66. Quoted in Curti and Carstensen, Vol. I, p. 716.

67. Fenster, p. 23.

68. Vivian Wood, "Helen Clarke and Social Work," in Swoboda and Roberts, Vol. I, pp. 67–69.

69. Langill, pp. 16–18; McBride, pp. 207–210.

70. Langill, pp. 16–18.

71. Langill, p. 22.

72. Langill, p.20.

73. In an essay whose title suggests the degree of this reverence, for example, Toni McNaron, one of White's graduate student during the 1960s, recalls her as "a beautiful, powerful, kind, brilliant woman," "The Purple Goddess: A Memoir of Helen Constance White," Women's Studies Research Center *Working Paper* #12, p. 2.

74. Helen C. White, Letter to Mother, February 27, 1921; Audrey Roberts, "Helen C. White Remembered," in Swoboda and Roberts, Vol. I, pp. 43–47.

75. Madeleine Doran, quoted in Laura L. Smail and Donna S.Taylor, "In Their

Own Words: Excerpts from Oral History Interviews," in Swoboda and Roberts, Vol. I, p. 126.

76. Smail and Taylor, p. 126.

77. Quoted in Smail and Taylor, pp. 127–128.

78. Smail and Taylor, p. 128.

79. Smail and Taylor, p. 128.

80. Barbara B. Pillinger, "Margaret H'Doubler: Pioneer of Dance," in Swoboda and Roberts, Vol. I, pp. 33–35.

81. Judith Mjaanes, "Women in the Art Department," in Swoboda and Roberts, Vol. II, pp. 79–81.

82. Ruth Dickie, "Women and Cooperative Home Economics Extension," in Swoboda and Roberts, Vol. II, pp. 89–91; Curti and Carstensen, Vol. II, pp. 404–406.

83. In 1927, the state's Normal Schools were given the power to grant bachelors' degrees in education and renamed the Wisconsin State Teachers Colleges; in 1951, their curricula were expanded to include the liberal arts and they were renamed the Wisconsin State Colleges.

84. Founded in the 1890s as the Stout Training Schools with an endowment from the State Senator after whom it was named, the school was reorganized as the Stout Institute, a two-year teacher-training school with an emphasis on "manual training" (later known as industrial education), in 1903.

85. Marcia Harycki, "Women in Industrial Education," in Swoboda and Roberts, Vol. I, pp. 85–87.

86. Ellen Last, "Voices from Three Generations of Women at Eau Claire: 1916–1970," in Swoboda and Roberts, Vol. I, pp.107–109.

87. For more information, see Frank A. Casell, J. Martin Klotsche, and Frederick I. Olson, *The University of Wisconsin-Milwaukee: A Historical Profile, 1885–1992* (Milwaukee: The UW-M Foundation, 1992); Elisabeth Holmes, "Women at the Extension Center in Milwaukee," in Swoboda and Roberts, Vol. I, pp. 89–92.

88. Jean L. Foss, "Emma Lou Wilder: She Came to Teach," in Swoboda and Roberts, Vol. I, pp. 53–55.

89. Langill, pp. 24–25.

90. Last, p. 107.

91. Buff Wright, "Women and Student Government," in Swoboda and Roberts, Vol. II, p.25.

92. Quoted in Langill, p. 27.

Chapter 2

Extension Leads the Way for Women

In 1906, a separate Extension program had been inaugurated at the University, relieving many faculty of the double duty they had long borne of teaching both regular and Extension courses; in 1914, the Agricultural Extension Service was established. A separate home economics program in Extension took over most of these outreach duties, under the new leadership of Elizabeth B. Kelley. Their programs drew more than 12,000 people from across the state to classes in cooking, farm institutes, and other short courses. When Kelley went to Washington, D.C. for special war duty in 1918, the position was assumed by Nellie Kedzie Jones, who accelerated program offerings during the war. Jones also coordinated the outreach efforts of many other faculty members from the Medical School, the Stout Institute in Menomonie, and the physical education department.[1]

During the next two decades, 67 of Wisconsin's 71 counties were reached by these Extension programs. More than 50,000 of Wisconsin's women belonged to the 3,000 homemakers clubs, in which courses were taught for women, by women, and about matters nearest to women's lives.[2]

The University of Wisconsin's Extension Division provided educational opportunities for women that marked a significant link between the early struggles for equal participation in higher education and the development of women's studies in Wisconsin. Many of Extension's most prominent women staffers were able to blend their service to women in education with larger political, economic, and social agendas in the women's movement on both the state and national levels, and that combination led directly to the women's studies courses that arose in the early 1970s.

* * * * *

The program that came to be known as University Extension grew out of several plans to extend the benefits of university training beyond the walls of the campus in Madison. The Regents initiated a series of "short courses" during the winter months, while the legislature believed that the state's farmers were in great need of agricultural education and thus developed the Farmers' Institutes, which brought the expertise of various professors to rural areas to lecture on farm problems, livestock management, dairy science, and a number of other practical topics.[3]

The concept of a university "extension" actually came from England, where universities were attempting to reach out to people who would never otherwise receive any advanced or specialized training. In the United States, several universities, notably Michigan and Pennsylvania, had set up successful farm institutes during the 1870s. Once the program was established in Wisconsin, it became enormously successful during its first ten years, with many thousands of farmers attending lectures on practical topics, as well as a sprinkling of liberal arts programs. In 1896, for instance, the Farmers' Institutes offered 57 two-day Institutes throughout the state.[4]

The Farmers' Institutes were supervised by the Farm Committee of the Board of Regents, and programs were developed as needed and evaluated according to informal measures of participants' responses. A second type of outreach program, the Mechanics' Institutes, were designed to serve the state's laborers, although these ultimately failed because the courses were not well-suited to the chosen audience.

* * * * *

Neither the needs of the state's female laborers nor the many women on Wisconsin's farms were considered at first, for all of these early courses were still presented only to a male audience. Farmers' wives either stayed at home tending the farm while their husbands attended the institutes, or came to the institutes purely to socialize. The awareness that these women might be a large potential audience for other specialized courses was slow to dawn. The voices of farm women were often lost, even in the decades of a renewed call for women's rights and women's suffrage at the end of the nineteenth century.

While still omitted from the rural outreach efforts, however, women were finally brought into Extension programming before the turn of the century. In 1887, the idea of offering special courses, seasonally, to teachers or librarians was first proposed and two years later, in 1889, the summer school for teachers became a formalized summer session at the University, bringing both men and women to the campus for classes in a range of subject areas. By 1908, the number of teachers enrolled had grown to more than 1,000 students from 221 only a decade before.[5] Other specialized summer programs which included women were soon added, including those for librarians, women in advertising, welfare service, nursing, journalism, dietary science, and secretarial work.[6] However, all of these courses were offered only to those already in professions and were given only in Madison, and not across the state.

Rural women were finally brought into the scope of the farm institutes beginning in the 1890s. Several outspoken farm women argued about the importance of dairying during the winter months. They maintained that women on the state's dairy farms should be trained in the fact that cows gave a greater milk flow during the winter, and the extra butter and cheese could be used as valuable supplements to farm incomes. As a result, several courses on winter dairying were added to the Farm Institute program. Soon these offerings were expanded to include other courses tailored to rural women, and in 1892 a series of Cooking Institutes was created.[7]

These institutes, specifically for women, were extremely successful. Each year after 1892, more than eleven cooking, canning, and gardening programs were offered, reaching thousands of Wisconsin women. The cookbooks from these institutes sold rapidly in printings of 10,000 at a time. In 1905, a women's course was added as part of the short course for farmers in Madison. The first session was led by Caroline Hunt in South Hall, and supervised by faculty who later formed the official home economics department at the University. Partly as a result of these successes, and in response to the growing enrollment of women students, the Home Economics Extension Department was officially organized in 1909.

During the next several years, these "schools of the skillet" were well attended and Extension's popularity among women across the state grew steadily. In 1914, the passage of the federal Smith-Lever Act provided for cooperation and funding from the federal Department of Agriculture working with state land-grant colleges and Agricultural Schools. At about the same time, the funding for Extension services tripled.[8]

Through this increased funding, county agents were hired to carry out Extension programs, including classes for women and girls. A speaker who addressed these agents in Madison argued that these courses for young girls and women in rural areas were crucial, even though the "best minds" had only recently "discovered that . . . the real cause of the exodus from farms is the discontent of farm wives and daughters."[9] Thus the Extension agents saw their role as educational, but with a higher social purpose—keeping Wisconsin's farms productive through working with women. Whether women's needs or the needs of the state should take highest priority was not questioned. No one involved in the program at the time perceived that women's educational needs might go beyond skills in homemaking. That insight was only to dawn several decades later.

An early Extension brochure reinforced this concept that helping women was only seen as a means to a wider social and economic end: "The great work of helping the women of our land [will contribute] to the material prosperity of the country and the general welfare of our farmers."[10] Wives as "helpmeets" remained the social ideal which guided educational programming.

Yet the popularity of the women's institutes was so great that in 1909, the new home economics chair, Abigail Marlatt, was paid at the top of the pay scale, $2,750 a year, and had a sizeable staff of assistants both in Madison and in the field. Women faculty from the University worked part time for Extension, along with women such as Nellie Kedzie Jones and Nellie Maxwell, who supervised the programs across the state. [11]

* * * * *

Many of the women faculty and Extension agents had a wider vision of the purpose of their labors, beyond sustaining the state's economy, and stressed the distinct value for the women themselves, including increased independence, a growing knowledge and role in citizenship, and the ability to work outside of their homes and understand the use of credit. County Extension agents worked alongside women in both farms and factories, assisting with training programs and bolstering the women's growing sense of independence. Courses in physical culture and fitness also appealed to women's changing needs. Many field agents led rural women in exercise classes, emphasizing fitness as a path to independence and health, and several Extension agents were also very active in the women's rights cause, spreading the ideals of self-sufficiency and the need for women's suffrage along with fitness routines and recipes.

Another impetus to the broadening curriculum came with the outbreak of World War I. Farm women had to take on many chores that were previously thought to be "men's work," just as women in cities entered factory work or even the nursing and ambulance corps. Extension agent Nellie Kedzie Jones had been a well-known and very outspoken women's suffrage worker and a vocal advocate of women's education. Jones came to Madison as State Leader of Home Economics in 1918, to take over leadership of the Home Economics Extension and to direct food programs such as wheatless, meatless, and sugarless days. She organized what was called the Women's Land Army, which mobilized Wisconsin women for war work of all kinds. Like many leaders in the national and state suffrage cause, Jones realized that education was a vital tool in the crusade, just as were efforts for the mobilization and organization of women. While the Women's Land Army worked for victory over the Kaiser, many Wisconsin women were enlightened through the efforts of Extension about the push for victories of their own.[12]

At the end of WWI, the passage of the federal suffrage amendment giving women the vote highlighted the need for practical citizenship training. Once again the Extension Division filled the need by offering courses for women across the state in citizenship skills, political debate, and public service. Even before the 19th amendment's passage, an advertisement in a Waukesha paper in May 1919 had announced a new course for women, "Citizenship and Government," being offered through University Extension. Waukesha was a hotbed of political activism in the suffrage cause, and the notice of the Extension course particularly called for "the attention of Waukesha clubwomen," many of whom soon also helped to create the Wisconsin chapter of the League of Women Voters, which grew directly out of the Wisconsin Women's Suffrage Association (WWSA) and the successful fight for suffrage.[13]

Citizenship education for both urban and rural women was offered along with courses for farm women in the economics of bookkeeping and household management. Extension staffers understood that these rural women needed skills in practical economics in order to survive the new market challenges for farm produce after the war and the changes caused when the agricultural depression of the 1920s vastly increased the migration from farms to cities. A sign of how deeply the women themselves valued the services Extension offered them, as well as of the importance of citizenship education, came when rural women successfully put the power of public petition to use after the war when the jobs of several of their favorite Extension agents were threatened.

Radio was also useful in broadcasting these messages about women's ability to organize, citizenship awareness in light of the suffrage cause, and related Extension offerings into homes served by electricity.[14] The development of the WHA radio station at the University in 1917, and its growing popularity after the war, provided a vital tool for programming. As radio came of age during the 1920s, and as farm homes were connected to electric lines, radio programs for women reached into the farthest corners of the state. Moreover, during the hard times of the Depression, the ability to use radio to help housewives economize and to share survival skills became even more essential. One of the most popular shows was hosted by Extension's Aline Hazard, whose broadcasts to rural homemakers during the 1930s received the greatest amount of fan mail of any WHA program.[15]

* * * * *

These individual courses were not the only work Extension performed for women in the early decades of the century. Another important contribution was the University of Wisconsin School for Women Workers, established in 1925, a summer program that brought forty "girls" from nine Midwestern states to Madison to study economics, English, and physical education, courses tailored "to the needs of working women." A three-month release was secured from their employers, their expenses were paid by a scholarship fund raised from organized labor, women's clubs, University alumni, and the YWCA, and the young women were housed on the Madison campus.[16] The women, most of whom had not completed high school, came from garment and shoe factories, knitting mills, packing houses, telephone offices, and other industries for six weeks of education and social activities. Noteworthies at the University met with the students, as did labor leaders such as Elizabeth Christman of the Women's Trade Union League.

The organizers hoped that these courses would enlighten the young women to make them better citizens and perhaps also make them better labor leaders. The purpose was not to wean them away from their work, but "to provide them a fuller and freer life,"[17] through an understanding of current events, workers' issues, and of themselves. The lecture style of teaching was taboo; classes were run in a discussion format and often held out-of-doors. The idea was to encourage the women to think for themselves and to translate that independence back to their communities, as leaders of women workers. Activities such as hikes and field trips were also part of the emphasis on fitness. Women graduate students helped to chaper-one the workers and lead informal discussions, and were available for counseling when necessary.

The program was expanded in 1928 to include working men and the name was changed to the University of Wisconsin School for Workers. Both women and minorities, particularly African Americans, continued to be strong components of the program throughout the next several decades of the school's operation, although active trade unionists formed the majority of students once the program became co-ed. The School for Workers encountered many obstacles from University administration in later years, including the suppression of the socialist beliefs of many in the labor movement during the 1930s,[18] and the autonomy of the women's program was curtailed. The school's first director, Alice Shoemaker, was demoted to a minor position, no longer able to perform her work independently, and budget cuts severely reduced staff and attendance until after the Second World War.

By 1950, in the midst of the post-war anti-Communist witch-hunt of McCarthyism, faculty with socialist leanings were cut from the roster and the Regents decided that the program should be more fully integrated into the University,[19] but the program itself survives to this day. The school also provided an important opportunity for a woman who would become one of the key figures in Extension's work for women: Marian Thompson worked her way through graduate school in the early 1940s by serving as one of the counselors. Thompson believed that her sense of solidarity with these young working women provided her with valuable insights for her later Extension work for women throughout the state.[20]

* * * * *

Extension's programs for citizenship took on a new patriotic emphasis with the entrance of the U.S. into World War II following the Japanese attack on Pearl Harbor in 1941. Leadership training and citizenship programs became very popular, and in 1943, the Extension Service became temporarily part of the War Food Administration.[21] Productivity was a top priority and many farm women left their homes to sign up for work in rural laboratories, testing breeding techniques and milk products for quality. Many others left their homes to move to nearby cities and live independently for the first time, entering factories and offices as they replaced men at war. The wartime wages provided some of them with financial independence for the first time, and the new cooperative housing arrangements brought them into close contact with other young women enjoying a new sense of freedom.

However, just as World War I veterans had expected women to leave campus after the war, American society expected its working women to give up their jobs at the end of World War II and settle down to make homes for returning soldiers. Many of these women resented being laid off and told that they had a new patriotic role which did not involve earning an income outside of the home. The women's movement had peaked with the passage of the suffrage amendment, and its rebirth in the postwar years came in part as a result of the greater wartime freedom many women had experienced and their bitter frustrations over layoffs and this forced return to the confines of the domestic sphere. Throughout the decade of the 1950s, many of them yearned for a way to better themselves, for an outlet outside their homes, or a return to school or job.

* * * * *

During the prosperity of the 1950s, the development of many labor-saving devices provided some women with more freedom, despite the changing cultural norms which began to mandate "more work" for homemakers to fill their leisure hours, with higher expectations in the realm of homemaking. The new electric inventions, including mixers, vacuum cleaners, and washing machines, and the success of rural electrification efforts meant that technology had come to rural areas as well as cities. Women welcomed new Extension courses about these inventions, and realized that housework did not have to be an all-day job; by the early 1950s, women began to have more time on their hands.[22]

The increased leisure time also allowed women to take special Extension courses in consumer education, insurance, wills, estates, and communication. Homemakers' clubs in rural areas grew up alongside the club movement in cities, as women continued their efforts to stay involved in their communities and to affiliate with other women outside of their homes. Extension agents continued to work with these clubs, offering programs on a variety of topics, ranging from the new science of freezing foods to discussions of women's role in public life.[23]

Extension agents not only helped to organize these homemakers' clubs, they also worked to establish a statewide network of women officers from each local group. All of these activities brought the benefits of association to women through affiliation with a statewide network. During the 1948 celebration of the Wisconsin centennial, many of these clubs, from farm areas and from cities, were active in creating displays regarding women's roles in state history. Such involvement brought increased awareness of the changes for women over many decades. This activism, even in a celebration of history, drew more and more women into public roles.

Despite the prevailing myth that the factory workers of the war years now wanted only a home and family, the number of women working outside the home actually more than doubled during the 1950s. By the end of the decade, the Wisconsin State Employment Service reported that fully 34% of the state's women age 14 and older were employed outside the home. Many of these women had only waited to see their children enrolled in school before they returned to the labor force. Others found outlets in volunteering in various community causes. The number doing paid work would increase steadily throughout the next decade.[24] The work of Extension was pivotal in laying the groundwork for women's increased entry into higher education in Wisconsin in the early 1960s.

The ability of Extension to respond adroitly in offering courses suited to women's new needs was due to the county agent system. These agents were the "ears in the field," listening to women's voices and responding with reports to the central administration in Madison about new topics for courses. Between 1933 and 1936, nineteen Wisconsin counties employed county agents; twenty years later, by 1957, fully 67 out of the state's 71 counties had agents.[25] The reliance upon agents to test the waters was a pattern that had begun in the earliest years and continued into the 1950s and 1960s, when Extension updated its practical courses for women who no longer wanted just "schools of the skillet," but rather, help reentering the job market and dealing with the new realities of careers, fewer children, and full citizenship.

* * * * *

The pattern of practical adaptation to women's changing needs was demonstrated in Extension's work in the urban environment of Milwaukee. Since its creation in 1907, the Extension Center there had served the vocational and educational needs of its local constituency, particularly in the commercial training courses needed for many city jobs. In the ensuing years, specialized courses in social work, penology, business management, and high school equivalency training were added. Extension's downtown Milwaukee center reached into the heart of the city, offering remedial education, vocational counseling, and also liberal arts courses in a variety of subjects. When professors offered work in German philosophy or literature, the halls were crowded to overflowing with students. Many immigrant students voiced appreciation for courses in English grammar (an essential tool for advancement in business) and for courses in literature. They valued the sense of independence that came from free-flowing discussions where their opinions counted.

Many young women who flocked to these courses encountered stiff resistance from their families. The prevailing European immigrant culture did not approve of higher education for women. Most had left high school for work at age 15 or 16, turning their wages over to their parents for room and board until they married. Those who enrolled in night courses to improve themselves or enhance their vocational opportunities were thought to be taking money from their families.[26] Bringing these second-generation immigrant women into Extension programs provided them with an avenue to Americanization that increased their sense of independence as women, a development that ran contrary to the typical immigrant family structure. Dealing with their students' aspirations, which conflicted with their restrictive home environments, proved to be a continuing challenge for the dedicated Extension faculty. However, the women teachers became crucially important role models for the younger women, who soon learned that they could board away from home, earn their own incomes, and form their own opinions. Their involvement in Extension was a crucial part of their growing independence.[27]

* * * * *

Leaders in higher education were aware of the changing demographic patterns for women during the 1950s. In 1953, the American Council on Education established a Commission on Educational Opportunities for Women, which began a study of these changes. Not surprisingly, one of the findings was that many women who had received some college education had been forced to retreat to homemaking by the social pressures of the postwar period. However, they comprised a greatly underutilized national resource, an untapped pool of talent in American society.[28]

Four years later, in 1957, the Commission helped to sponsor a conference that sought to explore the educational needs of American women, particularly due to the interruptions in their paths to learning. Many women's colleges led the way in how their alumnae's lives had been affected by their educations and their ability to reenter the workforce after years spent in domestic labor. Betty Friedan's pioneering study, *The Feminine Mystique* (1963), drew upon this research and concluded that there was a huge wellspring of frustration among women of education and talent that might burst forth into open rebellion. That frustration, combined with many women's experiences in the civil rights and anti-war movements, eventually brought attention to the problems of women themselves.

A handful of women in the academic world were in a position to effect some early institutional momentum in this area even before the so-called Second Wave of feminism began in earnest. Throughout the 1920s and into the 1930s, more women had received Ph.D. degrees than ever before in American history. Many of these women chose careers within the academic world and remained single. In a number of academic institutions, the explicit prohibitions against married women working were very powerful, and for others, tacit restrictions were often just as effective. After 1930, fewer women entered graduate school or received professional degrees, but a small and dedicated coterie of women was in place as new demands for women's education arose in the 1950s and early 1960s.

Within the Agricultural Extension Service, one woman who recognized the growing need for professional courses, rather than just the traditional home economics programs, was Nellie McCannon, who joined the Department of Agricultural Journalism in 1953. McCannon utilized newspaper articles, radio, and television to reach out to women on issues of the day. In later years, she responded to the growing need for specialized training for women in journalism careers by offering special classes and a yearly seminar for Wisconsin press women.[29]

Another important Extension Division leader, Signe Skott Cooper, worked to establish the first continuing education program in the country for nurses in 1955. As Chair of the Extension Division's Department of Nursing, Cooper began to enlarge her department in order to bring hundreds of nurses back to campus for retraining and special programs. Her particular love was obstetrics, but her knowledge was broadly based on world-wide travels to many nursing centers. She also wrote manuals that were utilized across the country, including *Contemporary Nursing Practice: A Guide to the Returning Nurse*.[30]

Even more influential was Martha Peterson, who became Dean of Women at the University of Wisconsin in 1956. Peterson had graduated from the University of Kansas in 1937 and worked as an instructor in the mathematics department, even teaching Military Math to soldiers during the war. She was Dean of Women there, at work on a doctorate in counseling, and studying for her preliminary examinations when she was invited to interview for the deanship at Wisconsin.[31] The committee that selected her for an interview had been hand-picked by University President E. B. Fred, who was interested in promoting the education of women. Chaired by Milwaukee banker and University of Chicago graduate Catherine Cleary, the committee sought out Peterson because of her strong record at Kansas on behalf of women students. (Also active on the search committee with Cleary were Ruth Wallerstein, a professor in the English department, and Helen Laird, a member on the Board of Regents and mother of Melvin Laird, later Congressman and Secretary of Defense.[32])

Peterson came to Madison in 1956, a time when women were becoming increasingly active. Not only was there a strong group of professional women, but her predecessor, Dean Louise Troxell, had successfully worked with women students to encourage their interest in campus activism and in careers or graduate training.[33] They had also begun to occupy prominent positions in student government: Joyce Mickey (later Erdman), who was the first female president of the Wisconsin Student Association in 1946, was later appointed to the Board of Regents and became a staunch advocate for women's causes. Mary Williams, who was president of the WSA in 1948–49, also later became a Regent. When Peterson arrived at the University in 1956, the president of the student body was a woman, Helen Rehbein, and a 1957 study demonstrated the benefits of campus activism. Among women who had graduated between 1947 and 1950, those who had participated in campus activities, union membership, or student government had a higher employment rate than those who did not (for instance, 51% among union women, compared to only 14% for their non-union counterparts).[34]

Supporting women's leadership and applauding their achievements, President Fred noted the many changes for women during the 1950s. "The time has arrived," he wrote, "when American women should carry the responsibilities for developing their minds and utilizing their intellectual capacity." The responsibility, he argued, rested not just with administrators and professors, but with "the women themselves who must be convinced that the seeking of new goals in education will bear new satisfactions and strengths."[35]

Martha Peterson felt uplifted, not only by President Fred's support for women and student leadership, but also by the network of women faculty she found at Wisconsin. She joined a core of professional women that included Helen C. White of the English department, Elizabeth Brandeis (economics), Elizabeth McCoy (bacteriology), Ruth B. Glassow (physical education), Fannie T. Taylor (theater), Francis Zuill (home economics), Marge McLaughlin (nursing), Maxine Bennett (surgery), and many others. Along with several women from the Madison community, they formed a book club, the Browsers.[36] One of the reading group's chief virtues was that the women who gathered for discussions were at the top of their fields and represented a great diversity of disciplines on the campus and off. They formed Wisconsin's first postwar women's network, although their strength lay in their ability to inspire young women and to serve as powerful role models, rather than activism in specific political causes. Through her connections with these women leaders at the University and in Madison, Peterson gained insights into the possibilities for women in this scholarly community, and also became determined to do her part to promote opportunities for promising young women under her charge.[37]

However, Peterson soon discovered that the University had far to go to serve its women students and prepare them for a changing world. She also became aware of the growing need to include older women in some form of continuing education and although, as Dean of Women, she was not formally a part of the Extension Division, Peterson was eventually given responsibility for overseeing that programming.

Utilizing its network of agents around the state, Extension was able to supply vital demographic information which could be used on any of the state's campuses as they assessed the changing needs of their population. Peterson was particularly interested in a 1958 Extension survey of women constituents that sought to discover how best to meet their needs. The results were not surprising: A majority of respondents worked outside of the home on farms or in small towns or cities; an overwhelming number listed continued educational opportunities as one of their top priorities.[38]

The survey revealed that since only 35% of the respondents had completed four years of high school, the interest in continuing education in many academic areas was very strong. Margaret Browne, Assistant Director for Home Economics Extension, brought a new emphasis on practical courses for women such as insurance, civic problems, voting issues, record-keeping, and income taxes. However, as Peterson appraised the results, she concluded that there was a great need for campus-based, as well as Extension-based, courses for these women.

With the encouragement of University Vice President Fred Harvey Harrington, Peterson decided to initiate another Madison-based survey to build support for a continuing education program for women on campus. She hired both Ruth Doyle and Kathryn (Kay) Clarenbach—a woman who would soon become one of the key figures in the development of the continuing education programming that eventually led to the establishment of women's studies programs throughout the state. Clarenbach had been aware of a program called "The Minnesota Plan," which had already begun to bring older women back into the fold of the University of Minnesota, and she discussed its dimensions with Doyle and Peterson.[39]

It was a timely idea and the three women decided to try and develop something similar for the University of Wisconsin. In 1961, Peterson initiated an extensive survey, mailed to 2,600 wives of University faculty members and of doctors and lawyers in the city.[40] The survey—which Clarenbach later admitted "was a very elitist kind of initial outreach"—asked about their past education and about their current educational interests and needs. The three women and an assistant, Pat Tautfest, met in the evenings to shape the questions on the survey and used the small stipend of $500 from the Dean's budget to fund its mailing and compilation. More than 1,120 surveys were returned, a percentage that spoke volumes about women's interest.[41] The survey's results made it clear that women throughout the community felt closed out of further educational opportunities. More than 400 responded affirmatively to a question about whether they would like to be interviewed immediately about the possibilities of pursuing their education.

Peterson, Doyle, and Clarenbach took the results to Vice President Fred Harrington and obtained his permission to invite a consultant from Minnesota to campus to address a planning conference for continuing education for women. As they were leaving the meeting with Harrington, recalled Clarenbach, he stepped out into the hall and asked Peterson, "Say, Martha, have you got somebody on this full-time now?" To which Peterson quickly responded, "Yes, I'll take care of that." Clarenbach was drafted that afternoon as the full-time planner for the upcoming conference.[42]

Under Peterson's guidance Clarenbach began to plan a way to open the University's doors to older women, which included spearheading the efforts to get women accepted in various departments, find financial assistance, and even secure some childcare. In laying the groundwork for what would soon become a permanent program of continuing education for women, Clarenbach and Peterson wanted to tap specialists from around the country who were pioneering in this effort.[43] Accordingly, Clarenbach's first task was to organize a conference on the subject for February, 1962. Speakers included Dr. Virginia Senders, from the pilot program at Minnesota, and among the consultants were Dr. Esther Raushenbush, President of Sarah Lawrence College, which had opened a new program for returning older women.[44]

After the conference, Clarenbach began efforts to implement the plan to bring older women students back to the University, and within a few months, University President Conrad Elvejhem had decided to create a permanent position for Clarenbach, as Director of Continuing Education for Women. Although Clarenbach would be part of Peterson's staff in the office of the Dean of Women, she would also work closely with University Extension staffers Constance Threinen, in Madison, and Dorothy Miniace, in Milwaukee, drawing on their experience in working with non-traditional women students.

One of the first tasks facing Clarenbach in her new job was to make sure that various University departments would accept these returning women students, without imposing any penalty for their interrupted educations. She also worked to allow the returning women the option of flexible scheduling and part-time work, which would fit into their lives as mothers, or even as wage-earners. As Clarenbach described it: "Our task at the university became one of identifying barriers, finding those people with the authority to snip the red tape, explaining the need for new procedures or a different rationale, and gradually redirecting or expanding the scope of an entire range of university services."[45]

An important goal was to design a course specifically to serve as an introductory orientation for these returning women. This first four-session, non-credit course, designed by Mary Farrell, head of the Madison Class Office of the Extension Division, and offered in the summer of 1965, was entitled "Today's Woman in Tomorrow's World" and gave women an opportunity to explore their own career goals, take an aptitude test, and meet with a visiting counselor. More than 150 women signed up for the first session, a powerful indication of the fact that these courses explicitly designed to meet women's needs were long overdue.

Another series of courses, also tailored specifically for women, was offered by Extension management professor Alma Baron. Believing that women seldom rose to management positions because they were unsure of themselves in business, Baron offered courses such as "Women New to Supervisory Management." These courses, which were part of UW-Extension's prestigious Management Institute, reached out to women to inspire them to set higher goals and to give them the techniques to succeed.[46]

Baron focused on skills that women in business typically lacked, such as speaking before large groups, speaking before a male audience, the art of delegation, assertiveness, managing men who have never had a woman boss, and time management. Many of her graduates stayed in touch with her from their new positions of authority, to consult and to thank her for giving them the skills and the confidence to reach higher.[47] Baron's classes had long waiting lists, as women from around the country began to hear about the seminars. Several years after teaching her first course for women only, Baron decided to offer a similar course, but entitle it "Management Training for Men and Women," because she believed that men needed to gain skills to work with women managers, too. However, she found that at first she had only women enrolling; the men stayed away. Finally, she persuaded several men to enter the course and the word finally got out about its value for both genders.[48]

In 1974, after I became an assistant professor, I tried to convince my all-male colleagues to let me introduce a course on "Women New to Supervisory Management." I tried again and again and finally succeeded, overcoming the nay-sayers by sheer persever-ance. The first course of its kind in the nation, it continued to be offered four times a year—filling up—until the mid-'80s. I was the only female faculty member of the Management Institute in those days, but I was successful and made money so the males left me alone.

Interestingly, the first faculty committee I was appointed to was the social committee. I managed after a year to set up a succes-sion schedule so each male got a chance to "perform" in a "female" function.

—Alma Baron

Even with successes like Baron's, the idea of tailoring a course just for women, establishing women's fellowships, and counseling returning women students was often attacked. Clarenbach remembered instances of backlash against her efforts on behalf of these mature women. She would be cornered at social gatherings and confronted by husbands who asked, "What are you doing to my wife?" She also received calls at home and heard complaints about women who were neglecting their domestic chores because they were busy with classwork or a new job. Clarenbach's response was simple and she publicized it wherever she could. "Wisconsin and the nation," she wrote, "are critically short of brainpower. We can hardly afford to ignore the three million women college graduates in the nation who could make a professional contribution." She added: "A woman is not abdi-cating her responsibility in taking time for her intellectual development. We think such a woman is becoming a better wife and mother."[49] Undeterred by criticism, the group planned to expand its program to meet the growing demand.

Persuading the University's admissions team to accept older women was also a challenge. Many of the women who wished to return, whether for enrichment or for undergraduate and graduate degrees, had stopped their educations part-way through and had incomplete credentials, so the program offered ACT (college entrance) testing and extensive counseling services. Many of the women were not sure of their academic interests or talents; others needed job counseling and assis-tance with part-time employment so that they could afford tuition. Often

Clarenbach would meet with dozens of women each month, listening to their career and educational goals, and gradually she formed a file box listing their names and talents. Some were assisted in returning to school, but others, through Clarenbach's efforts, were able to find meaningful employment in Madison. At one point, she reflected that at least "three hundred women in the Madison community were employed at jobs they got through my office!"[50]

However, many women also had to rely upon University funding to pay their tuition. To meet this financial need, Martha Peterson, working with Clarenbach and Ruth Doyle, had proposed to Fred Harrington (who had become University President in 1962) the creation of a series of scholarships for women graduate students that would be offered specifically to returning women. They realized from their survey and interviews with many mature women that household budgets simply would not stretch to pay for university coursework. Harrington approved the idea and, with a three-year Carnegie Corporation grant of $90,000 (later extended another two years) and money from the University, scholarships were established for returning women students pursuing terminal degrees such as the Ph.D.

The program became known as the E. B. Fred Fellowships, after the former University President, and in the first fellowship cycle in 1963, 141 women applied for funding. A committee selected the yearly fellowship recipients (52 in all, during the five years the program ran), who received grants of up to $2,000 per year and the guarantee of flexible scheduling as they returned to school.[51] A high percentage of the E. B. Fred Fellows completed their degrees, and the E. B. Fred Fellowship program has been described as having the highest yield of degrees achieved for dollars expended of any fellowship or scholarship program at the University.[52]

The least successful of Clarenbach's efforts was the attempt to obtain funding for subsidized childcare facilities on campus. When three early attempts failed by 1966, the idea was postponed until an extended facility was added to the University's married student apartments at Eagle Heights in 1970. Another frustration was the opposition from some of the women faculty themselves to the returning mature women students. "Some felt that once a woman had chosen marriage, she had eschewed career and had no right to seek both."[53] Other faculty members simply felt that their role in educating the traditional undergraduate women was more important.

The Continuing Education program monitored admission, part-time schedules, funding, and career counseling for these returning women between 1963 and 1967. Even in its first semester, the fall of 1962, the numbers were impressive, with an increase of 17% in the enrollment of women over the age of 24. However, the statistics still showed that more than two-thirds of undergraduate students at UW-Madison—14,004 out of 21,733—were male.[54]

* * * * *

Clarenbach had met many women from all parts of the state and recognized Extension's historic responsibility to serve all citizens. "In keeping with the Wisconsin Idea," she wrote, "we propose that these programs [for returning women] be state-wide, wherever possible, and that full use be made of the Extension Division Centers."[55] Clarenbach, Connie Threinen, and Marian Thompson, also a member of the Extension staff, planned a series of conferences at Extension Centers (which included the sites that soon became the University's two-year Center campuses) around the state in March of 1963. Invitations were issued in each local area and the conferences consisted of programs about continuing education, job placement and counseling, and enrichment opportunities.

In Milwaukee, Dorothy Miniace was appointed to the post of Coordinator of Women's Education in October 1963. "Women should be encouraged to regard their educations as part of a life plan, not just as a few years," Miniace insisted. "If college is interrupted by marriage and children, it can be resumed."[56] A recipient of a Ford Foundation scholarship for graduate studies in 1959, Miniace had spent the early 1960s on leave from the University studying adult learning programs at Columbia University and travelling through Madrid, Rome, and Paris to view European programs on adult education. For this new project, she asked clubs in the Milwaukee community for scholarship funds for women returning to school, and one of the first responses came from the UW-M Women's League, which contributed $1,000 toward twenty scholarships for returning women students.[57]

Other outreach programs to older women were held at the Fox Valley Extension Center and what is now the University of Wisconsin-Green Bay. At both locations, the response was once again very strong; women flocked to the special course offerings, such as "Young Mothers Back to School" and "Exploring Your Future," and signed up in great numbers for job and continuing education counseling sessions. One highly successful course, called "Explorations," was presented through Extension by Jane LeDain at the Fox Valley Center, by Ione Brown in Green Bay, and by Kathleen Capwell at Racine-Kenosha (now UW-Parkside).

These courses also gave women an opportunity to participate in the early events of the new feminist movement. A session at the Wisconsin State University at Oshkosh in March of 1965 drew an enthusiastic crowd of women to hear Betty Friedan: "We are in the midst of moving ahead in this revolution of women in the American family . . . As women we cannot be content with token pats on the head. Although our rights were given to us many years ago, are we free and equal if our boundaries are home, children, church, the kitchen, and suburban volunteer work?"[58] Friedan emphasized that fulfillment must come from the women themselves. "Creating this new pattern means bridging the traditional with the new identification of women in society today," she added, and urged the undergraduate women in the audience to face the question of who they were and what they wanted to succeed at, besides marriage and motherhood.[59] Friedan's insistence that undergraduate women be included in consciousness-raising efforts did not go unheeded. Members of Clarenbach's Extension office realized that working exclusively with older women, while ignoring the undergraduates who were right on campus, was shortsighted.

In light of their recognition that undergraduate women needed attention, the team at the Extension Division prepared a packet in August 1963 that was sent to 1,200 women seniors on the Madison campus. In the envelope were materials with an incisive message. The memo included a statement about graduate study, a bibliography of overseas opportunities for learning, a questionnaire about vocational interests from the placement coordinator, and special materials from business and professional women's organizations. As with the program for older women, the seniors were urged to seek vocational or educational counseling assistance as they sorted out their future options.[60]

* * * * *

Most of the Extension staff felt that the counseling component of the program for adult students, as well as for undergraduates, was as vital as the coursework itself. Women who had felt silenced and stifled for many years wanted to be heard and helped to find their proper niche as they reemerged from their domestic cocoons. Yet, even with all of the preparation and sympathetic counseling, the returning women students were on their own when they walked into their first classes. Several recorded their reactions in order to help others who came later. One wrote:

> By the time the first day of school came, I had been tested and questioned so often I felt like a veteran. But where were those 3,000 students over 25? My classes were filled with sweet YOUNG girls and virile YOUNG men! The boys surveyed me, amused, and thought I was in my dotage; the girls believed me to be a new breed of pioneer woman blazing a trail of glory for womanhood. [But] Quit? Never, they'd have to throw me out.[61]

Realizing that these mature women students often felt isolated, the campus YWCA began a series of gatherings for women students over 25. The sessions were well-attended and meetings became a kind of early support group. Attendees varied in their career goals, their educational programs, and their life choices. The age range at the meetings was between 25 and 65, but the participants shared many of the same concerns about balancing the traditional expectations of their roles with their exciting new educational opportunities. In a similar fashion, the E. B. Fred Fellows began a series of their own brown-bag lunches to exchange experiences and encourage one another in their graduate courses.

Witnessing the enthusiastic response of the first women who entered the continuing education program, the Extension team planned a second conference, with an emphasis on professional opportunities for women. The keynote speaker was Esther Peterson, Director of the Women's Bureau of the U.S. Labor Department. UW President Harrington agreed to fund the conference, which was once again highly successful—although Clarenbach remembers people leaving the sessions to watch John Glenn's orbit of the earth, which occurred the same day.[62]

One of the most positive strategies of the conference resulted from a decision to invite a number of chairs of women's organizations from around the state to attend. At a special forum, Esther Peterson explained the Commission on the Status of Women, created in 1961 by President Kennedy and originally chaired by Eleanor Roosevelt, and encouraged those present to form their own state commission, an idea which gained momentum immediately.[63] It was Clarenbach's first success in blending the needs of the continuing education program with a larger political agenda for women.

For Clarenbach personally, the idea of such a commission was an enormously liberating one. Calling it a "gift from on high," she described her feeling of elation that women might be asked to form a commission directed to identifying and meeting their needs, instead of always asking "is it alright for me to take a job," or "may I take some money and use it for my education?" The commission could fill the gap by looking into questions of discrimination and suggesting remedies directly to state government.

Clarenbach seized the opportunity and went with several other Wisconsin women in March 1963 to visit Governor John Reynolds and propose the formation of a Wisconsin Commission on the Status of Women. Reynolds, who had always been a fan of the late national Commissioner Eleanor Roosevelt, gave the idea his immediate support. The team urged him to sponsor a statewide conference on the status of Wisconsin women, to discuss issues and analyze the report of the national commission, which was due out in the fall. They believed that a widely-attended meeting, bringing Wisconsin clubwomen, labor leaders, educators, and professional women together before the actual formation of a commission, would solidify the need for its existence and give it an immediate agenda.

Accordingly, in July 1963, Governor Reynolds announced the event, and the Conference on the Status of Women in Wisconsin was set to convene in Madison on November 23 and 24, 1963. However, the assassination of President Kennedy on November 22 interrupted. Many people had already arrived in Madison, and Clarenbach spent the day meeting them at the Wisconsin Center and explaining the postponement, while watching Vice President Johnson being sworn in on Air Force One.

By January 31, 1964, when the conference finally convened, the report of the Roosevelt-led Commission was available for use and discussion. The advantage of holding the conference prior to the establishment of the commission in

Wisconsin lay in the fact that the speakers and discussion sessions were able to isolate high-priority concerns which the state commission could then begin to address immediately. "We were light years ahead" of other states in this respect, recalled Clarenbach, who was named the Chair of the Wisconsin Commission on the Status of Women when it was officially created in May 1964.[64] The publicity which grew out of the statewide conference also gave a boost to the Commission's formation. Clarenbach's ability to accept the post while remaining active at the Extension Division was due to the talents and dedication of her colleagues Threinen and Thompson, both community activists,[65] and to the full support of the University and Extension administration. Serving in Extension and as Commissioner dovetailed perfectly.

In fact, the staff at the Extension Division became the *de facto* staff for the Commission, because the Governor and state legislature authorized only a pittance in funding its work. Far from operating the Wisconsin Commission on the Status of Women from her campus office covertly, Clarenbach received the open and enthusiastic support of the University administration for her work for women. The response was, "Yes, take this position. You can use your desk and your telephone and secretarial time, even occasionally a little travel money to get to a meeting because this is the Wisconsin Idea, that the resources of the university should be available across the state."[66]

In reality, Clarenbach, Thompson, and Threinen were making up their roles at the Extension Division as they went along, since their only clear mandate was to help women. As Clarenbach described it: "I've always had the great good fortune to be able to define my own job."[67] Under Clarenbach's leadership, the Wisconsin Commission on the Status of Women became the centerpiece for many of the reforms for women in Wisconsin and the research conducted by the Commission regarding women's issues brought new meaning to the ongoing efforts to bring older women back onto the campus and into social involvement. One of the first tasks undertaken was the matter of women's legal status and the issue of equal employment opportunities. The Commission gathered and publicized information across its wide network. However, as an official creation of the state, it was forbidden to lobby directly for change, a restriction that was often chafing.

Being Chair of the Wisconsin Commission also brought Clarenbach and her staff into close contact with those working on other state commissions. Soon these commissions began to schedule joint yearly meetings in Washington, D.C. At the third meeting in 1966, Clarenbach and other leaders, who were frustrated by the limitations of their state organizations and their inability to lobby, met in Betty Friedan's room to discuss the need for a national lobbying organization to speak for women. Their meeting resulted in the formation of the National Organization for Women, or NOW.

At the official organizing conference for NOW the following November, 1966, in Washington, D.C., the Wisconsin delegation of eleven, led by Clarenbach and Gene Boyer from Beaver Dam, comprised more than a third of the total of 27 who attended. At that official meeting, Betty Friedan was elected President and Kathryn Clarenbach Chair of the Board. As with her leadership of the Wisconsin Commission on the Status of Women, Clarenbach, backed by Thompson and Threinen, was able to coordinate much of her work for NOW out of her office at the University.

In addition to chairing the Wisconsin Commission for fifteen years, from 1964 to 1979, Clarenbach also spent eighteen months on leave from UW-Extension to plan the celebration of International Women's Year in 1977. While she was away, Threinen took over her post at the Commission, in addition to chairing the Wisconsin branch of the National Women's Political Caucus. Wisconsin women were well-represented at the National Women's Conference that met in Houston in November 1977.

* * * * *

In 1965, the merger of two divisions of Extension into one resulted in the transfer of Clarenbach's job into Extension where she, Constance Threinen, and Marian Thompson became a powerful coalition for women. Within a few years, as the new field of women's studies began to develop throughout the country, UW-Extension faculty began to offer courses on women—beginning in 1972, when historian Jane Schulenburg created the course "Women in History: From the Greeks to the Renaissance." This was the first women's history course to be offered at the University of Wisconsin and was taught as a UW-Extension "extended timetable" credit course. The lectures for Schulenburg's course were recorded and aired by the Wisconsin Education Radio Network (WERN). Schulenburg was also the co-author of a popular history correspondence couse entitled "The Woman in Western Culture," which incorporated the cassette tapes of these lectures.[68] This kind of outreach effort touched people in communities across the midwest and made many people aware for the first time of the importance of intellectual inquiry into the history, experiences, and changing status of women.[69]

In 1968, the Extension's "College Week for Women" had begun to change its focus. Instead of traditional programming, the leaders invited the Madison chapter of NOW to put on a slide show that highlighted issues such as sexual harassment, employment discrimination, and reproductive freedom. Some women were appalled, but many loved it and sought further information. The Extension Division also led the way in holding seminars on the significance of the national Equal Rights Amendment, which passed Congress in February 1972 and was ratified in Wisconsin in April—although the following year, Wisconsin voters turned down the state Equal Rights Amendment. Women leaders in Extension were among the first to realize that widespread public education about women's rights and women's issues was more necessary than ever.[70]

At the same time, Clarenbach, Threinen, and Thompson continued their community activism. This not only applied to Clarenbach's ongoing involvement with NOW, during part of which time Marian Thompson became chair of the Wisconsin Commission on the Status of Women. Thompson also served on a special committee, created by the Wisconsin legislature in 1971, which studied state statutes for evidence of sex-based discrimination and language. Threinen worked throughout the early 1970s as Wisconsin Chair of the Women's Political Caucus and used Extension as a tool to educate women about important issues which would impact their lives. Through the Caucus, Threinen worked on a 1972 report which compiled data on the voting records of state legislators regarding women's issues.

In 1972, a new UW-Extension department was created: Women's Educational Resources (WER), designed to address both "individual women and the institutions which shape and reflect our values."[71] The goals were to gain "equality in legal treatment, to eliminate sex-stereotyping, to improve the economic status of women through real affirmative action, to help women secure proper health care, childcare, and family planning information," all that was "essential to a realistic widening of women's choices." The program of WER was "statewide in scope . . . on every campus in the University of Wisconsin System [newly merged in 1971] and on the expertise and authority of many public agencies."[72]

Appraisals of Wisconsin's leadership in addressing women's issues, both on campus and off, have credited the team led by Kay Clarenbach at University of Wisconsin-Extension and its realization that the Wisconsin Idea allowed for educational reform and social change to go hand in hand. It was also Clarenbach who convened what would become the Association of Faculty Women, whose first meeting initiated an even more dramatic phase in the struggle for gender equality at the University of Wisconsin.

Notes

1. Ruth Dickie, "Women and Cooperative Home Economics Extension," in Marian Swoboda and Audrey Roberts (eds.), *Wisconsin Women, Graduate Schools, and the Professions*, University Women: A Series of Essays (Madison: University of Wisconsin System Office of Women, 1980), Vol. II, pp. 89–91; Merle Curti and Vernon Carstensen, *The University of Wisconsin: A History, 1848–1925* (Madison: University of Wisconsin Press, 1949), Vol. II, p. 92.

2. Dickie, p. 92.

3. Curti and Carstensen, Vol. I, pp. 711–718.

4. Curti and Carstensen, Vol. I, p. 713.

5. Curti and Carstensen, Vol. I, p. 734.

6. *Bulletin of the University of Wisconsin, Extension Division*, Vocational Conference Papers and Vocational Preparation (Madison: University of Wisconsin, 1913).

7. W. H. Glover, *Farm and College: The College of Agriculture of the University of Wisconsin, A History* (Madison: University of Wisconsin Press, 1952), p. 151; Elwood R. McIntyre, *Fifty Years of Cooperative Extension in Wisconsin, 1912-1962* (Madison, University of Wisconsin Extension Service, College of Agriculture, 1962, Circular 602), p. 169; personal communication, Shirley E. Johnson to Jacqueline Ross, March 19, 1999.

8. Frederick M. Rosentreter, *The Boundaries of the Campus: A History of the University of Wisconsin Extension Division 1885–1945*, (Madison: University of Wisconsin Press, 1957), p. 63.

9. Rosentreter, p.64.

10. Quoted in Rosentreter, p. 68.

11. Rosentreter, p. 71.

12. Ayse Somersan, *Distinguished Service: University of Wisconsin Faculty and Staff Helping to Build Organizations in the State* (Friendship, Wisconsin: New Path Press, 1997), p. 122.

13. "To Study Citizenship," *Waukesha Freeman*, May 8, 1919, p. 2; see also Genevieve G. McBride, *On Wisconsin Women: Working for Their Rights from Settlement to Suffrage* (Madison: University of Wisconsin Press, 1993).

14. Rosentreter, p. 78.

15. Rosentreter, p. 211.

16. John P. Troxell, "Wisconsin's Summer School for Working Women," *American Federationist*, Vol. 32, #10 (October 1925), p. 945.

17. Troxell, p. 943.

18. Ernest F. Schwartztrauber, "Education in Industrial and Labor Relations, University of Wisconsin School for Workers," *Industrial and Labor Relations*

Review, Vol. III, #4 (July 1950), p. 542; Ellen Langill interview with Marian Thompson.

19. Dagmar Schultz, "The Changing Political Nature of Workers' Education: A Case Study of the Wisconsin School for Workers," Ph.D. dissertation, University of Wisconsin-Madison, 1972.

20. Ellen Langill interview with Marian Thompson.

21. Schultz.

22. The assumption that women inevitably benefited from these labor-saving devices has come under investigation by scholars such as Ruth Schwartz Cowan in her book *More Work for Mother: The Ironies of Household Technologies from the Open Hearth to the Microwave* (New York: Basic Books, 1983). Cowan explores the possibility that these "labor-saving devices" actually led to higher expectations for women, since chores began to be expanded with higher, and often unrealistic, standards, such as sheets that were ironed, towels that were washed daily for the entire family, and so on. However, for women who did not conform to these new homemaking standards, there was less time devoted to housework, fewer hours spent with the smaller number of children, and therefore, a greater amount of time which could be utilized for education and self-improvement.

23. Schultz, p. 168.

24. Max J. Hays, Supervisor, Wisconsin State Employment Service, in report to Chicago Regional Conference on "The Changing Status of Women," May 1962, Women's Bureau, U.S. Department of Labor.

25. Dickie, p. 92.

26. Elisabeth Holmes, *The Urban Mission Anticipated: A Biography of the UW Extension Center in Milwaukee* (Milwaukee: University of Wisconsin-Milwaukee Foundation, 1976), pp. 40–41.

27. In 1956, the University of Wisconsin-Milwaukee was created through the merger of the Wisconsin State College in Milwaukee and the Extension Center. The Milwaukee-based Extension activities remained, as they had always been, under the purview of the University of Wisconsin's Extension office in Madison.

28. Catharine R. Stimpson with Nina Kressner Cobb, *Women's Studies in the United States: A Report to the Ford Foundation* (New York: Ford Foundation, 1976), p. 9.

29. Dickie, p. 97.

30. Anne G. Niles, "Signe Skott Cooper," in Andrea Bletzinger and Anne Short (eds.), *Wisconsin Women, A Gifted Heritage* (Amherst, Wisconsin: Palmer Publication, 1982); Signe Skott Cooper, *Contemporary Nursing Practice: A Guide to the Returning Nurse* (New York: McGraw-Hill, 1970).

31. Ellen Langill interview with Martha Peterson.

32. Ellen Langill interview with Catherine Cleary.

33. Ellen Langill interview with Martha Peterson.

34. Ellen Langill interview with Martha Peterson; Buff Wright, "Women and Student Government," in Swoboda and Roberts, Vol. II, p. 109.

35. E.B. Fred, "Women and Higher Education," University of Wisconsin-Madison Archives.

36. Ellen Langill interview with Martha Peterson.

37. Ellen Langill interview with Martha Peterson.

38. Ellen Langill interview with Martha Peterson; Rosentreter.

39. At the University of Minnesota, during the late 1950s, a program was initiated to bring older women onto the campus by offering special testing and counseling programs and reduced class schedules, as well as some financial aid. Ruth Doyle was the wife of a Wisconsin Circuit Judge and a community leader in her own right, active in many civic groups. Her work with Clarenbach and Peterson often included helping Madison women, many of them her friends, who had expressed a strong interest in furthering their formal education.

40. As Clarenbach later wrote, "Today we would shudder to think in terms of 'wives of'; in 1961 we neither shuddered nor had we yet developed other rosters of interested women," Kathryn F. Clarenbach, "Continuing Education, A Personal View," in Marian Swoboda and Audrey Roberts (eds.), *Women Emerge in the Seventies*, University Women: A Series of Essays (Madison: University of Wisconsin System Office of Women, 1980), Vol. III, p. 121.

41. Ellen Langill interview with Martha Peterson; transcript of taped interview with Kay Clarenbach, November 3, 1987, *Documenting the Midwestern Origins of the Twentieth-Century Women's Movement, 1987–1992*, State Historical Society of Wisconsin; "Report of A Survey of Selected Madison Women," in Kathryn Clarenbach Papers, University of Wisconsin-Madison Archives.

42. In many ways, Peterson's choice was ideal for the future of women at the University. Kathryn Frederick Clarenbach was a graduate of the University of Wisconsin who had been an undergraduate leader and active in many campus organizations. She had worked as a dormitory advisor during graduate school (where she met her future Extension colleague Marian Thompson) and received a Ph.D. in Political Science in 1946 before leaving with her husband, Henry G. Clarenbach, to teach and work in New York, Michigan, and St. Louis. Upon their return to Madison in 1960, Clarenbach had found herself in the same position as many women in the 1950s. She was at home raising three children and looking for a way to re-enter the work force or the academic world and fulfill the earlier promise of her education.

43. Ellen Langill interview with Martha Peterson; Clarenbach interview, November 3, 1987, *Documenting the Midwestern Origins of the Twentieth-Century Women's Movement*.

44. Clarenbach, "Continuing Education," pp. 121–122.

45. Clarenbach, "Continuing Education," p. 123.

46. Marion Mills, "Woman of Achievement," in *Faculty and Staff Information*, March 1977.

47. Ellen Langill interview with Alma Baron. Baron also established a course for those working in the media, particularly educational radio and television, utilizing the resources of the University's media system. Before she retired in 1985, Baron was part of an advisory group which set up what would become the Center for Women and Philanthropy in Madison (1989), which was founded to educate women in the constructive use of their donated charitable dollars.

48. Ellen Langill interview with Alma Baron.

49. "Housewives Go Back to College Classrooms," *La Crosse Tribune*, January 9, 1963, p. 2.

50. Clarenbach interview, November 3, 1987, *Documenting the Midwestern Origins of the Twentieth-Century Women's Movement*, p. 231.

51. Clarenbach, "Continuing Education," p. 125.

52. Clarenbach, "Continuing Education," p. 125.

53. Clarenbach, "Continuing Education," p. 122.

54. "UW Spurs Continuing Education for Women," *Milwaukee Sentinel*, September 2, 1962, p.3; "U.W. News," February 2, 1963; UW-Madison Almanac—1998.

55. Clarenbach, "Report of a Survey," p. 8.

56. "Education Counselor to Aid Adult Women," *The Milwaukee Journal*, October 2, 1963, p. 6.

57. "Scholarships Aid Women," *The Milwaukee Journal*, June 6, 1965, p. 6.

58. "American Women Urged to Fulfillment Through Creativity," in *Oshkosh Northwestern*, March 17, 1965, p. 1.

59. "American Women Urged to Fulfillment Through Creativity," p. 1.

60. "Kathryn Clarenbach, Special Project: The Education of Women," August, 1963, in Kathryn Clarenbach Collection, University of Wisconsin-Madison Archives, Memorial Library.

61. "Mrs. Co-Ed Back to College at 45," *The Wisconsin State Journal*, October 8, 1967, p. 4.

62. Clarenbach interview, November 10, 1987, *Documenting the Midwestern Origins of the Twentieth-Century Women's Movement*, p. 239.

63. Clarenbach interview, November 10, 1987, *Documenting the Midwestern Origins of the Twentieth-Century Women's Movement*, p. 240.

64. Clarenbach interview, November 10, 1987, *Documenting the Midwestern Origins of the Twentieth-Century Women's Movement*, pp. 245–246.

65. Threinen had come to the University from Mt. Holyoke College, and by the

time of her appointment, was already active in local women's groups, such as the League of Women Voters.

66. Clarenbach interview, November 10, 1987, *Documenting the Midwestern Origins of the Twentieth-Century Women's Movement*, p. 262.

67. Clarenbach interview, November 10, 1987, *Documenting the Midwestern Origins of the Twentieth-Century Women's Movement*.

68. Personal communication, Shirley E. Johnson to Jacqueline Ross, March 19, 1999.

69. Ellen Langill interviews with Marion Thompson, Constance Threinen, and Jane Schulenburg.

70. Ellen Langill interview with Constance Threinen and Marian Thompson; Marian Thompson, "On Wisconsin Women: A Chronology of Recent Highlights of Wisconsin's Women's Movement (1962–1972)" (Madison: Women's Educational Resources, 1977).

71. Thompson, "On Wisconsin Women."

72. Thompson, "On Wisconsin Women."

Chapter 3

Feminist Activism and the Beginning of Women's Studies

Just as the needs of older and returning women students helped to shape University of Wisconsin-Extension's programming in the mid-1960s, so, too, the growth in the number of women undergraduates gave them increasing visibility in campus politics and curriculum.[1] At the same time, the rise of feminist consciousness among students, faculty, and staff inspired new attention to issues about women's status—and eventually, in Wisconsin as around the country, to the development of an entirely new academic field, women's studies.

From its beginnings, the national women's movement saw education as a crucial area of struggle, with many studies, meetings, and publications devoted to investigating the biases of conventional curricula and scholarship, images of women in literature and media, and the status of traditionally women-dominated fields such as teaching, both in the schools and in institutions of higher learning. These feminist analyses were accompanied by demands for change, but the world of higher education was slow to respond. Even after the passage of the federal Civil Rights Act of 1964, whose Title VII prohibited discrimination based on sex, few universities took action to remedy even the most blatant instances of salary discrimination.[2]

Nevertheless, the mechanisms were now in place to combat that secondary status. One of the most important early successes of the National Organization of Women (NOW), which had been founded in 1966, was to persuade President Lyndon Johnson to add sex discrimination to his October 1968 Executive Order 11246, which prohibited federal contractors from discriminating on the basis of race, color, religion, and national origin. Taking the stipulations of the Executive Order seriously, Bernice R. Sandler of the Women's Equity Action League (WEAL) began the first sex-discrimination lawsuit against the academic world early in 1970. She also filed complaints with the Department of Health, Education and Welfare (HEW), the agency charged with the oversight of federal cases in the area of discrimination in educational institutions receiving federal funding, claiming discrimination against women in a number of high-profile universities—including the University of Wisconsin.[3]

At about this same time, national professional academic organizations also began to become active on behalf of their women members. In 1968, the American Association of University Professors (AAUP) revived its "Committee W" on the Status of Women in the Academic Profession, and that committee immediately cited several large universities for serious violations of federal guidelines and for having no adequate affirmative action plans to remedy their problems.

Women also began to organize within the groups that represented specific academic disciplines: The Women's Caucus for Political Science was formed in

1968, the Coordinating Committee for Women in the Historical Profession in 1969, and the Committee on the Status and Education of Women of the Modern Language Association (MLA) in 1969. The first MLA forum on the status of faculty women took place at its annual meeting in 1970, where members also presented inquiries into sex stereotyping and lectures on feminist criticism. Throughout this period, feminist activism among students, faculty, and staff was growing at the University of Wisconsin and at other state campuses. Although some of the earliest organizing events occurred in Madison, they had an almost immediate impact on women across what would soon become the University of Wisconsin System.

A key event came in July of 1970, when the UW-Madison received a visit from representatives of HEW's Chicago Civil Rights Office in response to the employment discrimination complaints that had been filed by WEAL's Bernice Sandler. The local complaints had been based in part on material published in the spring of 1970 by a group of activist Madison women, the Women's Research Group (WRG). Among the WRG members were several who would become prominent feminist activists on the Madison campus, including assistant professor of English Elaine Reuben, English department graduate student Susan Stanford Friedman, and Extension staff member Rena Gelman. Although the HEW team did not interview any of the women who had done this research, their findings nevertheless provided the support for HEW's rejection of the University's affirmative action compliance document, which had been hastily compiled two months earlier and which, the HEW report noted, lacked specific procedures for its implementation, employment and promotion goals, and target dates for compliance.

With the University on notice that it would have to do a far better job of answering the HEW complaint, local women activists recognized that they could take advantage of federal pressure to pursue their own goals of improving women's status at the UW. Kay Clarenbach, already an acknowledged leader in the women's movement, used the occasion of the HEW report to call for a committee of faculty women on campus, and although her earlier attempt to organize women faculty in 1966 had not generated much interest, this one drew a tremendous response.[4]

The first meeting of the group that became known as the Association of Faculty Women (AFW) was held in Madison in October 1970, attended by more than 50 women who shared a growing interest in the subject of sex discrimination, and those present included non-tenured faculty members, as well as lecturers both in traditional University departments and at Extension. Some of these women had already become active in the feminist movement and realized that this was the time to create a strong presence on the campus itself. Many were newly motivated by the fact that the absence of an organization of faculty women had been one of the excuses offered for the HEW investigators' failure to interview women in connection with the complaint against the UW.[5]

The official founding of the AFW in November marked the beginning of a new era, in which women faculty, staff, and students began to see themselves as a group with a specific set of concerns in common—especially their status as victims of discrimination.[6] Membership soon grew to over 100, and at its first weekly meetings, the group established committees to deal with the many issues confronting women faculty, staff, and students. One, led by Rena Gelman and Elaine Reuben, concentrated on the idea of specialized courses for women and soon established the first UW-Madison courses in what would come to be called women's studies.[7] Another committee concentrated on affirmative action issues, including pay equity, promotion, and hiring policies, and on the University's next response to HEW, due in January, 1971. AFW's research included collecting women's own stories about discrimination in order to try and figure out what patterns existed.[8]

In fact, both the University administration and AFW members were working steadily to prepare responses to the HEW complaint. Then, quite suddenly, just before the 1970 Christmas break, a contract from the physics department to hire a new faculty member was held up because it did not comply with HEW's affirmative action guidelines. Meeting with Robert Gentry (Associate Vice President from the UW System Controllers Office), a member of the physics department, and AFW members, Cyrena Pondrom, associate professor of English, drafted a document stating the University's position, a "Working Paper on the Issue of Equal Treatment for Professional Women at the University of Wisconsin."[9] The working paper was used to temporarily resolve the logjam regarding hiring for the specific physics position, and became the basis for the University's official document on affirmative action and a model for other campuses within the System.[10]

This did not, however, immediately resolve the problem of the University's failure to comply with federal guidelines for affirmative action. In early January of 1971, Chancellor Edwin Young selected Pondrom to join his office in the newly-created position of Assistant to the Chancellor in charge of affirmative action for women at the UW-Madison. Many AFW members resented the fact that the administration had not asked them to nominate a candidate, but had instead hand-picked someone, and even those who approved of Pondrom's appointment objected to the fact that her position was only half-time, rather than the full-time director with support staff the AFW had recommended.[11] These objections made Pondrom's job a difficult one from the very beginning, and heightened tensions within the AFW itself.

As the federal deadlines passed, the newly established University of Wisconsin System failed to meet the initial goals of having an affirmative action plan in place for every campus, but, with the HEW office in Chicago severely understaffed, Wisconsin's delays did not receive effective federal scrutiny after the initial investigation. Women throughout the state realized that it was up to them to push for solutions, rather than waiting for additional government pressure on the University. As Ruth Bleier, a UW-Madison neuroanatomist and one of AFW's founders, later wrote, "We realized early on that if there were going to be an affirmative action program for this university, AFW would have to create it."[12]

First, however, it was necessary to document the discrimination women experienced, and surveys that the AFW conducted on the Madison campus easily revealed just how badly faculty women fared in terms of both numbers and salaries. Overall, women comprised only 7.8% of the total number of full professors, and only 2.5% outside of traditionally women's fields such as nursing or home economics. There were only 157 women in tenure-track appointments, out of a faculty of more than 2,000; differences between salaries for men and women in some departments averaged as much $10,000.[13] Although Wisconsin's open records law required the state to make many salary figures available to the public, the AFW had to petition for missing information in order to complete the survey. In UW-Madison Chancellor Edwin Young's office, they were occasionally met with cooperation, but usually with delays. According to Jacqueline Macaulay, who had requested files and information from Young's office under the open records law, a "spy" in his office also reported to her about policy and suggested that information was being doctored before its release.[14]

The AFW's first goal was to have at least one woman faculty member in every department by the fall of 1971, but reality fell far short of that, as the group's survey made clear. Many members believed that this goal could be reached not only by hiring additional women faculty, but by transferring women already in departments from non-tenure to tenure-track positions. This would, however, necessitate a dramatic change in University hiring policies, requiring an open search-and-screen procedure and full publication of any available positions in a national forum, a process that was not then common.[15] Instead, hiring was often done through informal collegial networks, with candidates invited to apply or recommended directly through phone calls and letters to faculty members in comparably prestigious departments.

In frustration at the slow progress in meeting hiring goals, the AFW began to draft its own affirmative action program. This comprehensive, 75-page proposal, submitted to the University administration in 1972, contained a plan for women's studies courses, as well as recommendations for hiring, promotion, salary equity, grievance procedures, and governance participation for both women faculty and academic staff. It also dealt with issues for women undergraduate and graduate students in areas such as counseling, career development, and opportunities for physical education.[16]

The plan stated that "In no case should the deadline [for compliance with hiring goals] be extended beyond fall, 1972, unless there is convincing statistical evidence that no qualified women candidates exist within the discipline."[17] Because such "statistical evidence" about workforce participation was not yet routinely being compiled nationally, though, this meant that the AFW itself had to embark on a national survey of women recipients of Ph.D. degrees in all of the disciplines where women faculty would be sought by the University. An enormous expenditure of energy went into this research, carried out largely by a volunteer task force of the AFW led by Jacqueline Macaulay, a researcher in the psychology department.[18] To help facilitate this research, the Madison Chancellor's office stipulated that each department should supply a list of those graduate schools "from which it regularly hires." This list would be used to compute the number of women degree recipients from those programs who comprised the potential hiring pool.

The goals of increasing the number of women hired and of opening the hiring procedures advanced very slowly in the next several years. In fact, the lack of progress resulted in Macaulay's creation of a "Lead Laggard" award which they gave to departments that were noticeably slow in hiring women—a dubious distinction that Macaulay later recalled often went to the departments of chemistry and history.[19]

At one point, Macaulay recalled, she had "better data than the administration"—data she collected simply by reviewing administrative data and then calling the secretary of each department where the record was unclear. "I just asked the secretary who answered if there were any minority professors and who they were."[20]

* * * * *

As the process of creating an affirmative action plan progressed in Madison, women at campuses around Wisconsin took a step toward a statewide organization that was unprecedented anywhere in the country. The AFW's decisions to reach out to women faculty at campuses across the state, to assist them in creating similar organizations on campuses, and to link these groups into a statewide network of women ultimately strengthened their political power as activists.

Much of the initial work of uniting women on all campuses came from Ruth Bleier and Joan Roberts, both faculty members at UW-Madison and co-chairs of the AFW, who divided up their speaking and organizing tasks according to their individual personal styles and comfort levels.[21] They drove to each of the state's four-year campuses in the spring and fall of 1971 to meet area women and share information about discrimination and other problems. On these road trips, they spent many weekends gathering faculty and staff women together to discuss the problems with the University's affirmative action plan, and the progress toward the development of women's studies courses.[22] The trips, recalled Jane Ayre, a member of the Department of Rehabilitation Psychology and Special Education who sometimes joined Roberts and Bleier on later journeys, involved throwing a duffle bag into the back of Bleier's small sports car on a Friday afternoon for another weekend's drive to one of the campuses in the newly formed UW System.

Bleier and Roberts' trips followed the 1971 establishment of the Wisconsin Coordinating Council for Women in Higher Education (WCCWHE).[23] That group's organizing conference was attended by more than 100 women from nineteen campuses, two-year Centers, and UW System offices. Bleier reported with satisfaction that "many faculty women, previously working in isolation . . . returned to their campuses with some new insights, visions, or inspiration."[24] Still, notes Jacqueline Macaulay, some women were insulted by what they perceived as a condescending attitude from their UW-Madison colleagues, and felt that their own local organizing efforts were not being recognized.[25]

It is no coincidence that this occurred in 1971, the same year as the merger of the state's colleges and universities into the University of Wisconsin System. As Macaulay later wrote, the group's formation demonstrated the vision of the Madison organizers: "They could see that they were dealing with problems that pervaded the whole system and that they would do well to join with women from other campuses to fashion remedies for the whole system."[26] It was the first successful effort in the country to unify women activists on campuses statewide and because of its emphasis not only on University employment practices, but on developing women's studies courses and programs on each campus, it put Wisconsin in the forefront of the new field's development as well.

Like Kay Clarenbach and her Extension colleagues before them, WCCWHE members took the Wisconsin Idea—that "the borders of the campus are the borders of the state"—seriously, turning it to their movement's advantage. The broad goal of the WCCWHE was "the achievement of full equality for women in all areas of the UW System,"[27] and by its third meeting, in December of 1971, the group had formulated a specific set of aims, which included fighting for the success of affirmative action Systemwide, working for better counseling and financial aid for women students, and assisting with the growth and development of women's studies programs on every campus. To this end the first coordinators, UW-Madison's Joan Roberts and Annette Harrison from UW-River Falls (soon replaced, following Harrison's unexpected death, by Pat Clark, also from UW-River Falls), established a Systemwide communications network so that women on each campus could share news of their progress or setbacks and alert each other to important developments.

The WCCWHE immediately decided to hold monthly meetings on different campuses around the state. Agate Nesaule Krouse, the representative from UW-Whitewater, recalled these gatherings as not only socially, emotionally, and intellectually stimulating, but also empowering. Women shared their frustrations, camped out on the hostess' living room floor or in nearby motels on Friday night, and worked on agendas all day Saturday before adjourning for the long drive home. As with so many of the activities women undertook to develop and nurture feminist networks and to build women's studies, members of the WCCWHE contributed their labor and were seldom compensated for their mileage, meals, or expenses.[28]

Networking among themselves was not the WCCWHE's only strategy. One of their earliest initiatives was called "Take a Regent to Lunch." Members approached several Regents (though others avoided them) and met over lunch to discuss the most blatant problems of discrimination. Regent Joyce Erdman, recalled Jane Ayre, was particularly receptive to these meetings. (In fact, Erdman, who had herself been a student leader in the 1940s, became a long-time champion of women's rights within the UW System, and later chaired the 1980 Task Force on the Status of Women.) The WCCWHE plan to focus on the Regents stirred strong opposition and an angry backlash on the part of System administrators, who felt that they had been purposefully bypassed in this effort,[29] but feminists' efforts to lobby the powerful Regents also had a least one important positive result.

Even with the formation of the WCCWHE, the Madison-based AFW remained active. One of its earliest achievements came from a few sympathetic Regents who seconded the proposal for the creation of a statewide Office for Women that would assist in responding to the problems of discrimination and could act as a liaison between the women's groups on the many campuses and System administration. Early in his tenure, AFW members had met with new University President John Weaver, asking him to create a committee on the status of women at each campus and a central office to coordinate efforts against discrimination.[30] In March, 1971, Weaver directed the campus chancellors to review the status and salaries of women faculty and academic staff and to correct existing inequalities, and the final report, issued that November, indicated that women were not being paid salaries comparable to men in similar positions and with similar credentials. (Retroactive pay raises were not actually received until July, 1972.)[31]

Weaver responded with the selection of Marian Swoboda to head the office, and Swoboda, who had a Ph.D. in educational administration and business from the UW-Madison, saw her role as that of a listener who would report to Weaver about the problems of women faculty and staff members on each campus.[32] There was, however, some disagreement about exactly what Swoboda's role should be, for while she perceived her post as a lightning rod for women's issues, others argued that she held a seat of sufficient authority to be an active advocate for their issues and urged her to do more to help them.[33] (The reality of gender-based pay inequities came home in a bitterly ironic way in 1972, when it was discovered that Swoboda's pay was significantly below that of the man newly appointed to a comparable position as Assistant to the President for Minority Affairs.[34])

Even after extensive lobbying efforts, though, the AFW's ambitious affirmative action plan, which they had submitted to University administrators, was not adopted because it appeared too far-reaching and suggested too many budgetary and programmatic changes. The plan did, however, prove useful as a blueprint for the women's groups both in Madison and on many other campuses, and for the Systemwide WCCWHE, which submitted a proposal to the Council of University Chancellors in 1972. Among the highest-priority demands were the appointment of an affirmative action officer and committee on each campus, specific studies showing comparative men's and women's salaries, the setting of hiring and promotion goals and the establishment of a job clearinghouse, better grievance procedures, and advancement opportunities for classified staff.

The WCCWHE also voted to send a delegation to the next Regents' meeting to present these demands. The reception that greeted Ruth Bleier, Joan Roberts, and Pat Clark, the bearers of this proposal, was described as "dismal." At the June 1972 meeting of WCCWHE, the three characterized their reception by the Regents as a "spontaneous show of contempt." As Jackie Macaulay recalled, the chancellors seemed to view these women's issues as only short-term employment problems and not as a recipe for long-term and fundamental change.[35] At the same time, though, Roberts later also remembered it as an occasion for a great display of solidarity among the women of the statewide System, with some two dozen women from UW-Milwaukee, where the Regents' meeting was being held, attending in support of the group's presentation, "and the men snapped to when those women appeared."[36]

Regardless of the Regents' opinions, though, some federal pressure on the University continued, because HEW still awaited receipt of a Systemwide affirmative action plan. UW-Madison Chancellor Young had again been able to delay the University's response through a series of letters to HEW that both promised compliance and detailed the administrative difficulties of filing immediate documentation, and other campuses had followed suit.[37] In an effort to get HEW to return to Madison and carry out its promised full investigation, Pat Clark corresponded with the HEW office in Washington, D.C. on behalf of the WCCWHE, and was assured in June of 1972 that the delayed investigation of the entire University of Wisconsin System would go forward before the close of the year.[38]

However, when the System's affirmative action guidelines were finally published late in 1972, they were "subject to interpretation,"[39] leaving a wide margin for de facto non-compliance. It was three years before HEW began its extensive review of the complaints of discrimination and inequity within the University of Wisconsin System. By that time, another major focus of the women's movement at UW-Madison and at campuses across the System had moved to center stage: the push for women's studies.

* * * * *

The efforts to remedy women's secondary status as students and employees were accompanied by attempts to rethink the curriculum and pedagogies at the heart of the University's mission as an institution of higher education. This was a period of radical critiques of education and pedagogy, the establishment of "free universities," and demands from many student activists that the curriculum be made more relevant to their lives and political concerns. Women's studies courses began to develop in the late 1960s, as faculty and students worked to remedy the absence of information about women and women's experiences from most courses in the curriculum.

From the outset, women's studies activists disagreed about whether the primary goal of the new field was integration into existing disciplines and departments or the establishment of an autonomous interdisciplinary area of study. But while the tension between these two approaches continued to be a central issue in women's studies over the next two decades, all agreed about the ultimate goals: both correcting the scholarly biases of the traditional disciplines and discovering or recovering information about the history, experiences, and perspectives of women, which had been excluded from the existing curriculum and from predominant research paradigms. Thus, women's studies developed both through feminist revisions of existing courses and through the establishment of new ones. According to one study, more than 100 Women's Studies courses were offered at universities in the United States during the fall semester of 1970. Many of these were isolated, often non-credit courses taught by faculty as an overload to their regular teaching. One year later, the number had grown to more than 600 courses at more than 200 U.S. colleges and universities.[40]

Wisconsin campuses were among the early sites of women's studies, with the first courses being developed during the 1969–70 academic year. Chapters 4 and 5 discuss the development of the state's first women's studies courses at University of Wisconsin campuses in Madison, Milwaukee, Whitewater, Oshkosh, and Green Bay, and the establishment of the System's earliest women's studies programs at these pioneering institutions. What began as a group of feminist volunteers teaching courses like Madison's "Alice in Academe" grew, by the mid-1970s, into collections of courses that challenged traditional knowledge and produced innovative new research, and prompted the University of Wisconsin System's Vice President of Academic Affairs to appoint a statewide task force to investigate the feasibility of setting up women's studies programs in every University of Wisconsin institution.

Notes

1. The enrollment of women students in what became the University of Wisconsin System more than doubled in the six years between 1966 and 1972, and increased to more than 72,000 (of 147,934 total students) by 1978; *The University of Wisconsin System Fact Book, 1998–99*, p. 31.

2. The last-minute insertion of Title VII into the Civil Rights Act was made by several Southern Senators, supposedly as a ploy to defeat it. Much to their surprise, and that of the country, the act passed with Title VII intact. The debate over the strategy of the Southern Senators continues in a discussion over whether acknowledging their action tends to deny the long struggle of women's rights activists to achieve such civil rights legislation for women, a struggle which dated back to the suffrage movement nationally. There is also disagreement about whether the addition of Title VII might actually have been sincere: "The limited evidence available indicates that the crucial margin of victory was supplied by Republican Congressmen who supported civil rights, not Southerners who opposed the bill. These Members most likely voted for 'sex' as a surrogate for the ERA, on which they had been lobbied for years, and as a response to testimony on sex discrimination in employment which they had become aware of through this lobbying and through hearings on the Equal Pay Act the year before." Jo Freeman, "How Sex Got Into Title VII: Persistent Opportunism as a Maker of Public Policy," available at <http://www.inform.umd.edu/EdRes/Topic/WomensStudies/ReadingRoom/>, reprinted from *Law and Inequality: A Journal of Theory and Practice*, Vol. 9, No. 2, March 1991, pp. 163–184.

3. Mariam K. Chamberlain, *Women in Academe, Progress and Prospects* (New York: Russell Sage Foundation, 1988), p. 15.

4. Ruth Bleier, "History of the Association of Faculty Women-Madison," in Marian J. Swoboda and Audrey J. Roberts (eds.), *Women Emerge in the Seventies*, University Women: A Series of Essays, Vol. III (Madison: University of Wisconsin System Office of Women, 1980), p. 11.

5. Bleier, "History," p. 11.

6. Bonnie Cook Freeman, "The Women's Movement and the University," in Swoboda and Roberts, Vol. III, pp. 1–9.

7. Ellen Langill interviews with Rena Gelman and Elaine Reuben.

8. Bleier, "History," p. 11.

9. Ellen Langill interview with Cyrena Pondrom and Constance Threinen; draft copy, "Working Paper on the Issue of Equal Treatment for Professional Women at the University of Wisconsin," in Women's Studies Consortium Collection, University Archives.

10. "Working Paper on the Issue of Equal Treatment."

11. Bleier, "History," p. 12.

12. Bleier, "History," p. 13; Ellen Langill interviews with Jane Ayre, Cyrena Pondrom, Jacqueline Macaulay, and Diane Kravetz.

13. Bleier, "History," p.13.

14. Ellen Langill interview with Jacqueline Macaulay. This "spy" was a woman, still unnamed, who worked as a high level secretary in the office. As Macaulay later reported, she offered evidence that files had actually been "cleansed" before they were released to her; personal communication, Jacqueline Macaulay to Laura Stempel Mumford, March 21, 1999.

15. Ellen Langill interview with Cyrena Pondrom.

16. Bleier, "History," pp. 12–13; "An Affirmative Action Plan for the University of Wisconsin," AFW Files, University Archives.

17. "An Affirmative Action Plan for the University of Wisconsin"; Ellen Langill interview with Jacqueline Macaulay.

18. Ellen Langill interview with Jacqueline Macaulay.

19. Ellen Langill interview with Jacqueline Macaulay.

20. Personal communication, Jacqueline Macaulay to Laura Stempel Mumford, March 21, 1999.

21. Personal communication, Joan Roberts to Laura Stempel Mumford, March 12, 1999.

22. Ellen Langill interviews with Jane Ayre and Joan Roberts.

23. The WCCWHE was named for the Wisconsin Coordinating Council for Higher Education, an organization that had served a coordinating function among Wisconsin's state colleges and universities before the 1971 merger that created the University of Wisconsin System.

24. Quoted in Jacqueline Macaulay, "A History of the Wisconsin Coordinating Council of Women in Higher Education," in Swoboda and Roberts (eds.), Vol. III, p. 24.

25. Personal communication, Jacqueline Macaulay to Laura Stempel Mumford, March 21, 1999.

26. Macaulay, "A History," p. 24.

27. Macaulay, "A History," p. 23.

28. Ellen Langill interviews with Agate Nesaule (formerly Krouse) and Jane Ayre.

29. Ellen Langill interview with Jane Ayre.

30. Bleier, "History," p. 12.

31. Freeman, p. 3.

32. Ellen Langill interviews with Marian Swoboda and Audrey Roberts.

33. Ellen Langill interviews with Jane Ayre and Audrey Roberts.

34. Macaulay, "A History," p. 28.

35. Macaulay, "A History," p. 27; Ellen Langill interview with Jacqueline Macaulay.

36. Personal communications, Joan Roberts to Laura Stempel Mumford, November 11, 1998, March 12, 1999.

37. University of Wisconsin, Association of Faculty Women Minutes, Meeting March 20, 1972; "TAA Efforts for Women Get Strong Backing," *Capital Times*, March 22, 1972, p. 12. As a result of the delay, and based on a number of grievances which had been filed, AFW decided to join the Equity Action League in a lawsuit for the equity raises. The suit was finally settled in 1973 with a token pay adjustment for faculty women at UW-Madison, which later proved to be woefully inadequate.

38. Letter to Pat Clark from J. Stanley Pottinger, Director, Office of Civil Rights, Department of Health, Education and Welfare, Washington, D.C., June 13, 1972, in University Archives.

39. Macaulay, "A History," p. 28.

40. Barbara Scott Winkler, "A Comparative History of Four Women's Studies Programs, 1970 to 1985," Ph.D. dissertation, University of Michigan, 1992, p. 3.

Chapter 4

The First Women's Studies Courses

A lthough the University of Wisconsin-Madison was not the first state campus to develop women's studies courses, it was the site of much of the early organizing around feminist issues, and eventually became the home of the UW System's largest women's studies program. As a major center for the student anti-war movement, Madison was filled with politically aware women who, like feminist activists around the country, began in the late 1960s to view their own experiences through radical political lenses. Even seemingly innocuous rules were capable of arousing vocal and highly politicized reactions, as happened in the spring of 1970, when a storm of protest greeted the administration's decision to maintain parietal rules for women living in campus dorms. At the same time, faculty and staff were organizing to combat specific forms of discrimination in the workplace, and as Chapter 2 illustrates, a considerable amount of innovation in women's education had already taken place at the University, especially through Kay Clarenbach's work in Extension. The demands for change in workplace conditions and other aspects of the campus climate were always linked to demands for new courses and research on women, but it was in this period that the quest to establish women's studies began to require graduate students and faculty to identify some of their academic concerns as separate from other issues of discrimination, affirmative action, and so on.

A highly visible leader among graduate students in 1969–1970, Susan Stanford Friedman ascribed her conversion to campus-based feminist activism to an incident that occurred in the English department. A fellow graduate student, Barbara White, had begun to apply for teaching jobs at several universities across the country during the spring of her dissertation defense. Not only was she summarily turned down by the schools, one department had the boldness to write her that they were not interested in a *woman* even with such outstanding qualifications. White made more than 200 copies of this response, circulated them around campus, and called a meeting that led to the founding of the Women's Research Group. The wording of this job refusal was, Friedman later recalled, a wake-up for other women graduate students, who would soon be in the same position of looking for jobs in a market where male applicants were openly preferred.[1]

One of the most dramatic events of 1970, which involved Friedman directly, occurred when members of the activist Women's Research Group (WRG) discovered that a planned Women's Day program, to be held at the Wisconsin Center, featured only male speakers. Although Kay Clarenbach's office was not responsible for organizing the event, it was one of the sponsors, and WRG spokeswoman Elaine Reuben called Clarenbach to say her group would like the opportunity to have a table in the lobby to hand out their pamphlets. WRG also got approval for two members, Friedman and Jan Roache, to be allowed to speak for five minutes each to offer a woman's perspective at the close of a session on "Marriage on the Rocks," being conducted by a male psychotherapist, Carl Whitaker, a pioneer in the field of family therapy.[2] However, on April 21, when Friedman came into the hall, she was denied admission to the lecture. Telling the plainclothes policemen that she had been approved as a respondent, Friedman pushed past them and took a seat, which she then had to cling to when the police approached her. Despite the previous agreement to let her speak, Friedman—who was pregnant at the time—was pried from her seat and carried out of the hall, to the cheers of most of those in attendance. She was beaten before being taken to jail, where she was charged with disorderly conduct. Her husband posted bail, and Friedman was released the same evening.[3]

Horrified at the police behavior and dismayed that the agreement with Friedman's group had been undermined, Clarenbach and Connie Threinen met with her the next morning. They assured her that they had not ordered the response and handed her a prepared statement to read, which Friedman rejected, preferring to speak for herself. She later pled guilty to a greatly reduced charge, but the incident provoked a lot of press coverage, and one of the Madison daily newspapers, *The Wisconsin State Journal*, called Friedman a "semi-martyr to the cause of women's liberation."[4]

A report written by Threinen, Marian Thompson, and Clarenbach emphasized the fact that Friedman was released because she had done no harm. In fact, plainclothes policemen had been stationed at the Wisconsin Center (where the event had been held) and campus police chief Ralph Hanson had apparently suggested a "preventative arrest" in case any disruption was planned. (The overreaction of the police, Friedman later discovered, may also have been due to the fact that, just two months earlier several campus radicals had used red spray paint, to symbolize menstrual blood, to put feminist slogans on Alumni Hall.) As seasoned feminist leaders themselves, Threinen, Thompson, and Clarenbach demanded that the University respond to the unjustified incident by "giving immediate and serious evidence of addressing itself to eliminating its discrimination against women."[5] However, the administration provided no such response, and women's outrage at their treatment escalated.[6]

The anti-war protest movement on the UW campus was more subdued following the 1970 Kent State killings and the death of a graduate student in the bombing of a campus building in Madison. However, feminist activism—which was partially a reaction to the sexism of the left as experienced by women activists in both the civil rights and the anti-war movements—continued to fill the campus, and the growing evidence of sexual discrimination added fuel not only to the anger of the faculty and staff members who were beginning to organize into the AFW, but to the growing militancy of graduate and undergraduate women students. One participant recalled the academic year 1971–72 as the point at which "the anger and discontent of women reached the explosive stage," with events that included both positive developments (such as Joan Roberts' new course on "The Education and Status of Women," described later in this chapter) and negative ones, including a volatile May 1972 sit-in by women students protesting their exclusion from a committee on equity in graduate student appointments.[7]

During this period, women graduate students formed the Graduate Women's Caucus, paralleling the organization of the Association of Faculty Women (AFW), undergraduates formed the Women's Action Movement (WAM), and women academic staff members began the Madison Academic Staff Association (MASA). While these groups functioned separately, they united in issuing demands and staging rallies to publicize them. Almost every weekend during the early 1970s, there was a march to the state capitol, where speeches about women's issues from abortion rights to rape counseling were given to enthusiastic crowds. Diane Kravetz, a new assistant professor in the School of Social Work and a WRG member, recalled taking the speaker's stand on more than one occasion, finding a new voice within herself that spoke for women's rights.

The concerns of students, faculty, and staff often overlapped, and one aspect of discrimination that became a source of action for all of them was the enormous discrepancy in budget and facilities between men's and women's athletics, a concern that in fact dated back to the 19th century. There were no real gym facilities for campus women, and the so-called Red Gym—the University's main athletic building—was male only. One particularly dramatic protest occurred on February 25, 1973, when a group of activists (including Rena Gelman, Ruth Bleier, and future UW-Madison Dean of Students Mary Rouse) entered the Red Gym and jumped into the pool during the male-only nude swim. (Three of the bravest even took their clothes off in joining the men!) Madison newspapers had been alerted to the plan and the incident made headlines. By the fall of 1973, the Red Gym was available for both male and female students, though not equally. In December, 25 women students and several faculty "liberated" the gym itself when they marched onto the basketball court during a men-only practice to emphasize the inequity in the hours allotted to men and women. They then hung a large banner over the gym, proclaiming "Brought to you by the Women's Sports Liberation Alliance."

In a similar incident, women who had protested to Athletic Director Elroy Hirsch that they had no locker rooms at the Memorial Shell, the physical education facility that contained the indoor track, took his lack of response as a signal to move in. Armed with sheets, these women—including Ruth Bleier—marched into the men's locker room, hung up the sheets as a divider, and proceeded to change and shower. Hirsch quickly found a way to put showers and changing facilities for women into the Field House next to the football stadium.[8]

While these protests did achieve important and immediate results, however, equity for women athletes was extremely slow in coming, even with the pressure imposed by the federal government through Title IX, the provision of the 1972 federal Higher Education Act prohibiting discrimination against women. Despite Title IX's mandate, it would take more than 20 years for women's intercollegiate sports to approach even numerical equity with men's (with eleven programs for each by 1997).[9]

* * * * *

While protests over athletics and women's inclusion in public events like the Women's Day program were going on, Madison faculty and students were also beginning their struggle to establish women's studies courses on campus, a goal that was frequently listed among the corrections feminists demanded in their critiques of women's status in the University.

In 1971, members of the WRG created the campus's first course in the field of women's studies. Called "Alice in Academe," it was offered as part of Contemporary Trends, an experimental interdisciplinary program at the University, which allowed 1- or 2-credit topical courses to be offered on faculty overload to freshmen and sophomore students. The "Alice" course was team-taught in the fall of 1971 by members of the Women's Research Group, with the faculty sponsorship of Diane Kravetz. It was repeated each subsequent semester for several years, becoming for many students an introduction to women's studies because it touched on many women-centered topics in a variety of disciplines.[10]

Alongside "Alice," another course was developed in the Law School, with some financial support from the local Bar Association. Entitled "Law and Contemporary Problems: Women and Law" and taught by Linda Roberson and several other lawyers and law students, it was first offered in the fall of 1971 amid controversy about the topics it covered, including lesbian issues. At about the same time, an annual Women and the Law conference was also planned for Madison at which lesbian issues were prominent, and the confluence of these events led to the withdrawal by the Bar Association of its offer to fund Roberson's course. The course was only rescued from extinction by the sponsorship of Law School professor Stuart Macaulay, the husband of AFW activist Jackie Macaulay.[11]

The first regularly listed, full-credit, academic course in women's studies at UW-Madison was created by Wisconsin Coordinating Council (WCCWHE) president and AFW activist Joan Roberts. Roberts' idea, which proved enormously successful, was to invite women from disciplines across the campus to offer lectures in a course entitled "Women in Higher Education," which she described as "a collective effort of faculty women." The first problem she encountered was finding at least one woman representative from each discipline. "What followed," she wrote, "was an exhaustive search . . . nevertheless, only one of the twenty-nine women refused to be involved in the new class."[12] At first many of these women, scholars in their own disciplines, claimed that they "had no special knowledge of women from their own intellectual perspectives." Roberts' terse reply to them was, "Who else does?" From this coalition of women emerged a dynamic course, which challenged the intellectual assumptions of both its students and its teaching faculty, enrolled heavily, and was repeated for several semesters.[13]

Following the success of Roberts' course, many women faculty were able to offer women's studies courses based on work in their own disciplines. Several of these courses were taught through Contemporary Trends, which meant that the instructors were not compensated for their overload work. Annis Pratt, tenured in 1973 in the English department, had joined the Executive Committee of the Contemporary Trends Program in 1974 and raised the issue of remuneration. Pratt argued that these courses had already raised $88,000 in tuition credits for the University and that the teachers should be paid. The University's response, Pratt later recalled, was to "partially fund the xeroxing and film costs of courses in Contemporary Trends."[14]

Pratt also recalled that during her own semester of teaching a Contemporary Trends course called "Herstory: The Changing Role of Women in Society," the focus, typical for the era, was a negative one. "We heaped bad news upon our students from the first day," Pratt later wrote, emphasizing the stereotyping of women in literature, the "problem that has no name" (Betty Friedan's term for women's frustration over the limits they faced), and other examples of discrimination against women, without, as she admitted, "going on to explain how women can empower themselves." Texts tended to be either by or about "women who went mad, committed suicide or were seriously depressed"—*The Awakening* by Kate Chopin, *The Bell Jar* by Sylvia Plath, *The Yellow Wallpaper* by Charlotte Perkins Gilman, *The Golden Notebook* by Doris Lessing.[15] Nevertheless, while women's studies practitioners eventually came to recognize the importance of balancing analyses of women's victimization with information about women's successes, students in the early courses, many of whom who had never before encountered stories like these, were empowered by what they learned about women's lives and struggles.

Stimulated by the overwhelming enrollments in these first courses, women faculty began to create new courses in their own departments, such as "The Biology and Psychology of Women," team-taught through Contemporary Trends by Ruth Bleier, medical historian Judith Leavitt, and psychologist Marjorie Klein. In 1972–73, several department and divisional committees approved courses with a focus on women, including the School of Social Work course "Professional Problems: Sexism" and the English department's "Women in Literature." The following year, Diane Kravetz developed the course "Sexism and Social Work Practice" in response to the requests of women students in her department as well as her own work for Roberts' course. Course offerings grew substantially during the 1973–74 academic year, a campus survey showing that there were more than 38 such courses—an expansion almost beyond the wildest dreams of the AFW committee three years earlier.[16] But it was an incident involving academic employment, rather than curriculum development, that provided the final spur for women to demand a program in the new field of women's studies.

Despite the success of the "Women in Higher Education" course, Roberts herself ran into political problems over tenure in 1973–74. When she came up for tenure, its denial—despite excellent teaching recommendations, on such the grounds as the characterization of her scholarship as not "of the right kind"— proved to be a lightning rod for feminist anger on campus.[17] Roberts appealed the decision and her charismatic leadership aroused many graduate and undergraduate women students to action on her behalf.

Both friends and foes from the AFW came to her appeal hearing, held in a large campus auditorium. On the stage were the male members of her department who had denied her tenure and in the audience were hundreds of women, most irate over what they perceived to be injustice. The white lights shone down on the men as they reviewed the reasons for her denial, largely based on their assertion of a lack of proven scholarship. When a department member accused Roberts of lying about a book contract, one of her students left the room, called Roberts' publishers, returned to the hearing with the phone number, and suggested he call himself.[18]

However, despite this showdown, Roberts lost her appeal. In complete frustration, hundreds of women students marched in protest up Bascom Hill to register their anger in front of the administration building. Their outrage spilled over to expressions of fear that Roberts' denial meant the end of women's studies offerings on campus and an implied threat to other non-tenured women who dared to challenge traditional approaches to scholarship and pedagogy. Their fears were partially justified, since another early feminist activist, Elaine Reuben (who went on to become the president of the National Women's Studies Association), had been denied tenure by the English department in the fall of 1972.[19] (A year after her own tenure denial, Roberts also left Madison to teach at Syracuse University, publish her book, *Beyond Intellectual Sexism* [1976], and continue her appeal in court.[20])

Women across the state supported Roberts, and the Madison protests were a powerful reminder of the strength of women's solidarity. Diane Kravetz notes that the formation of a women's studies program on the UW-Madison campus was stirred, at least in part, by the students' outrage and the escalation of militant protests over these tenure denials,[21] although it would take a Systemwide Task Force on Women's Studies to actually establish the program itself. In the meantime, women on several other University of Wisconsin campuses had also been organizing around the same academic issues and working hard to develop new courses and, in Milwaukee, even a women's studies program.

* * * * *

The **University of Wisconsin-Milwaukee's** efforts to establish a women's studies program began with great energy in the fall of 1971, coinciding with an important national women's studies conference at nearby Alverno College. At the conference, representatives from campuses across the country spoke of their fledgling courses for and about women and their struggles to enter the academic mainstream with the creation of a systematized women's studies curriculum. That same year, it actually became possible to major in women's studies through the UW-M College of Letters & Sciences' committee interdisciplinary major.[22]

In December 1971, Lenore Harmon, Leila Fraser, Rachel Skalitzky, Edith Bjorklund, and Angela Peckenpaugh organized a core of faculty women into an informal feminist group called the Committee on the Status of Women, or CSAW (pronounced "seesaw"). Like Madison's AFW, CSAW supported both affirmative action programs for hiring, promotion, and pay equity for women, and the creation of a full women's studies program at the UW-M. By the next semester, Spring 1972, there were women's studies courses in several departments, including Elsa Shipman's course "Women in Literature," and Ethel Sloane's "Women and Biology" (Sloane's original title, "Women and Their Bodies," had been vetoed by her department).[23]

Women's studies supporters had been distributing a mimeographed sheet listing all the courses with women's studies content, and by the end of 1972 they were included in the University's official course schedule; by then there were 40 listed, and 53 by the following spring. CSAW tried to ensure that only courses that had 50% or more of their content focusing on women were included as women's studies courses, but members soon had to begin visiting classes after discovering that some male professors were submitting their courses for inclusion on the list, claiming a women's studies component, merely to build their enrollments.[24]

The UW-M faculty had several crucial advantages in their attempts to establish a formal women's studies program. First was the fact that Lenore Harmon and Leila Fraser, both activists on behalf of women's studies, were already in positions of authority in the Chancellor's and Vice Chancellor's offices, Harmon as Advisor to the Chancellor on the Status of Women, and Fraser as Assistant to the Vice Chancellor for Affirmative Action. Second, committee member Edith Bjorklund was the head of Acquisitions in the UW-M library, which made it far easier to promote the growth of the women's studies collection, which would provide the necessary intellectual resources to carry out feminist research and teaching.[25]

Vice Chancellor William L. Walters already believed in the academic importance of a women's studies program, and Chancellor J. Martin Klotsche quickly approved the CSAW proposal, incorporating funding for an office and a half-time coordinator, Lenore Harmon, into his budget for the Spring of 1973. With a basic structure established, the University of Wisconsin-Milwaukee was able to boast that it took only one year from its first list of courses in the spring of 1972 to the creation of a separate Women's Studies Program with its own office in Bolton Hall in the spring of 1973.[26] This remarkable achievement made the UW-Milwaukee the first in the System to create such a program, one of the earliest in the country. By the fall of 1973, a survey revealed that there were more than 2,000 women's studies courses being offered nationwide, but only 80 formally organized women's studies programs.[27]

Despite this early success, Harmon recalled some of the early pitfalls in working to create an integrated program and offer a certificate in women's studies (which didn't occur until 1976). One challenge was to continually provide more courses to meet the growing demands. The listed courses were so popular that the enrollments soared and waiting lists often existed. Second, the program wrestled from the outset with the difficult question that had plagued the field of women's studies from the outset: Did they want women's studies to become a separate discipline unto itself, or were they instead seeking the full integration of women's experiences and questions about women into the major disciplines?

The Women's Studies Committee—then the program's governing body—chose the second alternative, and Harmon and her successor as coordinator, Rachel Skalitzky, worked with the steering committee to visit departments and encourage the development of significant feminist courses within each discipline on the UW-M campus. This process of curriculum transformation proved to be enormously difficult to achieve, since departments agreed to offer courses on women, but not to alter their existing materials based on the new knowledge. Although most of the major disciplines have since incorporated feminist critiques and analyses into their curricular and research paradigms, 25 years later this continues to be a source of conflict, not only within women's studies, but between women's studies and more mainstream academic departments at UW-M and elsewhere.[28]

As had always been the case, the struggle for feminist influence on the curriculum occurred alongside other feminist campus efforts. CSAW continued its work on affirmative action issues, often in collaboration with women from around the state. (Lenore Harmon recalled a significant visit to UW-M by Cyrena Pondrom in the fall of 1972 to discuss the HEW investigation and to urge the faculty women at UW-M to orchestrate a response, as had their counterparts at Madison.[29]) In 1975–76, CSAW was part of an official task force to complete a University-wide study of compliance with Title IX, the Federal legislation prohibiting discrimination, which had been mandated by the Higher Education Act of 1972. During this process, the women of CSAW learned about the continuing pay inequities, the difficulties of promotion and tenure for faculty women, and the continued underrepresentation of women in many departments and in the hiring process. Their report, typed on an old typewriter in the hot summer of 1976, was submitted to the University's new Chancellor, Werner Baum, but the recommendations were never implemented.[30]

Disappointed but not discouraged, the women realized that, to effect the changes they wanted to see, they needed to understand and be part of the University's power structure, so they set out to learn its rules of governance and join its inner circle. Through monthly meetings, they began quietly organizing to get members of their group elected to previously all-male divisional committees and to the powerful Faculty Senate and University Committee.[31] One of CSAW's early initiatives was to take a resolution to a College of Letters and Sciences faculty meeting, mandating that women be hired at the University "in proportion to the percentage of women students enrolled."[32] This proposal aroused a stormy response among the faculty. The meeting was packed, and one male professor asked in anger: "Do you want to turn this university into just a women's college?"[33] Still, while the formal proposal failed to pass, and despite similar expressions of anxiety from those whose power was threatened, the group's goals were clear—more women had to be hired—and they had become a campus force to be reckoned with.[34]

* * * * *

A much smaller campus than either Madison or Milwaukee, the **University of Wisconsin-Whitewater** experienced a somewhat different pattern than its larger neighbors. A core of women faculty there were able to take advantage of the size of their campus and their access to the administration to bring women's studies into focus before many other campuses in Wisconsin. In fact, UW-Whitewater offered some of the first women's studies courses in the state, although their program was not formally established until 1975.

As early as the fall of 1969, Agate Nesaule (then Krouse), a member of the English department, offered a course in American Studies entitled "Women in American Culture," which focused on women's historical experiences and particularly on several women writers. A second course, taught by Barbara G. Taylor (then Desmarais) in the fall of 1970, was entitled "Women in Literature, Feminist Re-evaluations" and had the subtitle "Suicide and Madness." An early visit to the Whitewater campus by UW-Madison assistant professor Elaine Reuben was one of the sparks that ignited local women to do additional organizing, conveying what Taylor recalled as a sense of mission and an experience of bonding between women at different campuses.[35]

A key event in the early development of women's studies as a new interdisciplinary field, and in the development of UW-Whitewater's women's studies program, was the first national conference on women's studies held at the University of Pittsburgh in the fall of 1971. Out of this conference came *Female Studies*, one of the first academic women's studies publications, and soon after this, the Feminist Press was established by Florence Howe and Paul Lauter. Three interdisciplinary journals in women's studies appeared in early 1972, *Women's Studies*, *Feminist Studies*, and *Women's Studies Newsletter*, and three years later, the journal *Signs: Journal of Women in Culture and Society* was inaugurated.[36] With these journals, the spread of knowledge in the new field accelerated and course syllabi were even traded from campus to campus. Women's studies was emerging as an interdisciplinary field in its own right, drawing its strength from the combined intellectual forces of many disciplines as they asked a new set of questions about subject matter pertaining to women.[37]

For Agate Nesaule, the conference heightened her enthusiasm about teaching women's studies and about creating a full program on the Whitewater campus. While several members of the administration opposed her, the faculty in English and American Studies agreed that her course on "Women in American Culture" was valuable. Students flocked to enroll, encouraging other faculty members to begin to offer similar courses, including "Women and Literature," "Women and Politics," "Women in Sociology," and "Educating Women and Girls."[38]

Many women from the community of Whitewater also enrolled in these courses, and the faculty took the initiative very early in bringing community women into their program and in offering outreach programs with a broad appeal, such as a "Workshop in Women's Studies" in the summer of 1972, part of the campus's Continuing Education Program. This course was an introduction to women's studies tailored for high school teachers who wanted to bring the new field back to their schools. Nesaule and Taylor also traveled to churches, women's groups, and schools, presenting programs and distributing materials on women's studies.[39]

When I remember the very first years of women's studies at the University of Wisconsin-Whitewater, in the late 1960s, I always think of the talks that Agate Nesaule and I gave at junior high and high schools, and at meetings of women's church groups, book clubs, and even sewing circles. Women of all ages and backgrounds were curious and interested. They wanted us to explain this simultaneously exciting and threatening new phenomenon called the women's movement, and many of them wanted us to help them think about ways that women's studies could be introduced to younger women, their students and daughters.

Because women had just begun to wear trousers in business settings, and because Agate and I wanted to discourage people from stereotyping feminists, if one of us wore pants, the other always wore a skirt. Five years later, neither of us had a skirt in her wardrobe! And I think now about how naïve our careful costuming was, and how strangely antiquated it would seem to the current generation of feminists.

—Barbara G. Taylor

* * * * *

Another campus to establish a successful early series of women's studies courses was the **University of Wisconsin-Oshkosh**. Student support for women's studies at UW-Oshkosh did not develop as early as on some other System campuses, and Barbara Sniffen recalled that when she first became the faculty liaison to the campus's Associated Women Students in the late 1960s, the group's members were organizing a program with models for a bridal show, like many women students around the country who hadn't yet begun to reexamine traditional extracurricular activities.

But by the early 1970s, the climate on campus had changed, due in part to the efforts of a small core of women students, and when the first women's studies courses were offered, there was a receptive and growing audience. Courses on "American Political Institutions: Women's Rights," "Feminist Consciousness in Literature," and "Sex Differences in Society" were offered under a "Special Topics" rubric in the Fall and Spring of 1971. By the following academic year, a number of additional "Special Topics" courses were added, as well as more courses in specific disciplines, including "Women's Liberation and Literature" and "Special Problems: Images of Women in Modern Drama."[40]

Plans for a more coherent set of courses were developed by a Women's Studies Committee, appointed in the Fall of 1972 by the Dean of Letters and Science. The committee's recommendation, adopted by the Faculty Senate, was for an interdisciplinary minor in women's studies to be established as soon as two more courses were added to increase the list of offerings. By early 1973, an ad hoc committee had prepared a detailed proposal for this minor and when the two necessary courses were offered in the Fall of 1974, the minor was formally approved. The UW-Oshkosh proposal—described as the "first [interdisciplinary certificate] curricular planning document of its nature in the public universities of Wisconsin"—was historically significant not only for women's studies, but for the development of interdisciplinary studies around the state, and the minor was the first to be offered in women's studies at any UW System campus.[41]

Evidence of how active women students had become came in 1974, the same year that the minor was approved, when students lobbied for a place of their own on campus. They received approval for a small third-floor room to use as a women's center, but the room was located in the administration building and did not provide the casual, welcoming, walk-in atmosphere the students had sought. The women's center was unwillingly moved several times, making it hard for women to find it, and finally found a home in the basement of the Student Union. The women students felt pushed around,[42] and did not think that the space or location were adequate for their needs and for the personal and confidential counseling they wished to offer, and since the women's studies program also had no autonomous space, it could offer them little help.

* * * * *

The early effort to create Women's Studies courses at **University of Wisconsin-Green Bay** was more similar to that at UW-Whitewater than at UW-Oshkosh. However, at Green Bay the energy propelling the courses and program came from an even wider mixture of community women and students, as well as faculty. Existing for 20 years as a two-year Extension Center before its conversion to a four-year campus in 1968, UW-Green Bay had already established itself as a haven for the non-traditional students from the community. A core of students and community women, many of them adults returning to school, brought a high level of commitment and involvement to the UW-Green Bay experience. Moreover, the existing interdisciplinary nature of the school's academic programs allowed for the relatively smooth creation and development of the interdisciplinary field of women's studies.

The first proto-women's studies course offered at UW-Green Bay, "Marriage and Family," appeared in the fall of 1969, making it one of the earliest in the state. Its creators described the course as a "theoretical and empirical analysis of one of the major institutional structures of American Society, the family, [and] not a course on 'how to be happy although married.'"[43] Another early course, offered in 1970, was entitled "Fertility, Reproduction, and Family Planning," and included a consideration of reproductive physiology, fertility control, and human sexuality. After several successful semesters of this course, a student-led committee created a supplementary one, "Our Bodies, Ourselves," based on the ground-breaking women's health book of the same title. This course covered women's health-related issues from birth control to abortion, as well as other topics connected to women and their bodies, such as lesbianism and rape, and provided an avenue for women to discuss such issues openly.[44]

One of the first women involved in the Green Bay program, English professor Estella Lauter (now Chair of English, UW-Oshkosh), has attributed its success to a very cohesive group of faculty who were hired in the 1970s—including Bridget Mugane (who probably lost her bid for tenure because of her commitment to the new field), Julie Brickley (who died in 1998), Wava Haney, Sidney Bremer (now Dean at UW-Marinette), Lynn Walter (now Professor of Social Change and Development), and Lauter.[45] Brickley, Bremer, Walter, and Lauter chaired or co-chaired the women's studies Program Committee in rotation without release time or secretarial support from 1977–1993, providing consistency and clout to the program as they received tenure. Carol Pollis, who had taught courses on the family and participated in early discussions of the minor, provided assistance in defining the first women's studies position after her promotion to Associate Dean in the 1980s (she is now Dean of Liberal Arts and Sciences).[46]

As at UW-Oshkosh, the activism of students and local women helped to build UW-Green Bay's feminist community, creating the first women's center on a University of Wisconsin campus in 1974. This center was staffed by a paid half-time director and christened the Lucy Stone Center, after one of the earliest U.S. crusaders for women's rights. The center provided a campus home "where the political, expressive, and academic directions of the feminist movement could come together in one space."[47] For six years, until it was closed by the Chancellor in 1981, the center provided a site where community women, students, and faculty could come together to create a day-care facility, a rape counseling program, and a resource library stocked with feminist books, films, and periodicals. As Lauter recalled, the women "even decorated one room of the center's most spacious and effective location as a womb to which we could retreat from the chillier aspects of the University's climate. And, of course, we hammered out the contours of the academic program there."[48]

* * * * *

Although these early efforts to establish women's studies programs and courses occurred on separate campuses of the University of Wisconsin, they did not occur in isolation, either from one another or from national developments. The first national conferences such as those at Alverno College and the University of Pittsburgh, the emergence of new academic journals, and the development of nationwide networks of women's studies teachers and students, made the work of building local programs easier, as did the growing connections among campus-based feminists around the state of Wisconsin. As the 1970s continued, those statewide connections would develop into a formal organization fighting for improvements in women's status within the University—and would eventually lead, in 1974, to a UW Systemwide Task Force recommending that women's studies programs be established at every campus in the state.

Notes

1. Susan Stanford Friedman, Oral History Project interview, 1978, UW-Madison Archives.

2. Connie Threinen, Marian Thompson, Kathryn Clarenbach, "Report on Women's Day Incident," to Wisconsin Center Advisory Committee, May 26, 1970, University of Wisconsin Archives.

3. "The Women's Research Group and Ed Friedman both arrived at jail to post bail. Ed 'won' that battle." Personal communication, Susan Stanford Friedman to Laura Stempel Mumford, February 19, 1999.

4. *Wisconsin State Journal*, Sunday, August 9, 1970, Section 1, p. 12.

5. Friedman later recalled that at the time, she had little respect for these older feminists, who were of a different generation than the activist campus group to which she belonged. Confessing her ignorance at the time about Extension's many accomplishments for women, Friedman acknowledged that within only a few years, as she moved from graduate student to staff and then faculty member, she came to hold them in the highest regard for their significant pioneering efforts; Ellen Langill interview with Susan Stanford Friedman.

6. Threinen, Thompson, Clarenbach, "Report on Women's Day Incident."

7. Jane Van Dyke, "Graduate Women Assess the Campus: A Case in Point about Sexism," in Marian Swoboda and Audrey Roberts (eds.), *Women Emerge in the Seventies*, University Women: A Series of Essays (Madison: University of Wisconsin System Office of Women, 1980), Vol. III, pp. 40–41.

8. *Wisconsin State Journal*, February 26, 1973, p. 1, and December 3, 1973, p.1; Ellen Langill interview with Rena Gelman.

9. Kit Saunders, "Women's Athletics at Madison and Title IX," in Swoboda and Roberts, Vol. III, pp. 81–92; Marilyn Skrivseth, "The Evolution of the Wisconsin Women's Intercollegiate Athletic Conference from 1971 to 1993 as Experienced by the Primary Women's Athletic Administrators," Ph.D. dissertation, University of Iowa, 1995; "Title IX," *On Wisconsin*, September/October 1997, pp. 16–21.

10. Ellen Langill interviews with Rena Gelman, Diane Kravetz, and Susan Stanford Friedman.

11. Ellen Langill interview with Jacqueline Macaulay; personal communication, Jacqueline Macaulay to Laura Stempel Mumford, March 21, 1999.

12. Joan I. Roberts, "Ramifications of the Study of Women," in Joan I. Roberts (ed.), *Beyond Intellectual Sexism: A New Woman, A New Reality* (New York: David McKay, 1976), p. 3; Ellen Langill interview with Joan Roberts.

13. Roberts, "Ramifications," pp. 3, 4; Leslie Gail Rothaus, "The Women's Studies Program: A Case Study of the Political Survival of a Nontraditional Program Within the University of Wisconsin-Madison," Master's thesis,

University of Wisconsin-Madison, 1980, p. 69.

14. Rothaus, p. 72.

15. Annis Pratt, "Imploding Marginality: Women's Studies and Me," unpublished essay, p. 12.

16. *Final Report of the System Task Force on Women's Studies*, September 30, 1974, p. 27.

17. Ellen Langill interviews with Joan Roberts, Jane Ayre, Annis V. Pratt, Evelyn Torton Beck, and Elaine Reuben; personal communication, Joan Roberts to Laura Stempel Mumford, March 12, 1999.

18. Personal communication, Joan Roberts to Laura Stempel Mumford, March 12, 1999.

19. Personal communication, Susan Stanford Friedman to Ellen Langill, September 23, 1998.

20. Roberts' case advanced through the local and state courts, and the Wisconsin Education Association contributed $10,000, while NOW and other national professional organizations backed her in other ways. She did eventually receive a settlement from the UW, recalling that "it was necessary to settle because of the personal difficulties of others in my life." Despite the trauma of this experience, however, Roberts went on to have a highly successful academic career, serving on the faculty of SUNY and Syracuse University, completing at least four books and eventually retiring in the late 1990s. Personal communication, Joan Roberts to Laura Stempel Mumford, March 12, 1999. See also Sarah Slavin Schramm and Jacqueline Macaulay, "Joan Roberts vs. the University," in *Rocking the Boat: Academic Women and Academic Processes*, ed. Gloria DeSole and Leonore Hoffman (New York: MLA, 1981).

21. Ellen Langill interview with Diane Kravetz.

22. Rachel Skalitsky, "The Women's Studies Program—Milwaukee," in Swoboda and Roberts, Vol. III, p. 60.

23. Ellen Langill interview with Ethel Sloane.

24. Ellen Langill interviews with Ethel Sloane and Rachel Skalitsky.

25. Ellen Langill interviews with Ethel Sloane, Rachel Skalitsky, and Lenore Harmon.

26. Skalitzky, "The Women's Studies Program—Milwaukee," p. 59; Ellen Langill interviews with Lenore Harmon, Rachel Skalitzky, Ethel Sloane, Jane Crisler, and Edith Bjorklund.

27. Barbara Scott Winkler, "A Comparative History of Four Women's Studies Programs, 1970 to 1985," Ph.D. dissertation, University of Michigan, 1992, p. 4.

28. Ellen Langill interviews with Lenore Harmon, Ethel Sloane, and Rachel Skalitzky.

29. Ellen Langill interview with Lenore Harmon; additional materials in the UW-

Milwaukee Women's Studies Archives.

30. Ellen Langill interview with Jane Crisler; Jane Crisler, "Committee on the Status of Women at Milwaukee," in Swoboda and Roberts, Vol. III, pp. 35–38.

31. Ellen Langill interviews with Ethel Sloane and Rachel Skalitsky.

32. Ellen Langill interviews with Ethel Sloane and Rachel Skalitsky.

33. Ellen Langill interviews with Ethel Sloane and Rachel Skalitsky.

34. Ellen Langill interviews with Rachel Skalitzky, Ethel Sloane, Jane Crisler, and Lenore Harmon.

35. Ellen Langill interview with Barbara G. Taylor (formerly Desmarais).

36. Catharine R. Stimpson with Nina Kressner Cobb, *Women's Studies in the United States: A Ford Foundation Report* (New York: Ford Foundation, 1986), p. 22.

37. Stimpson, p. 22.

38. Ellen Langill interviews with Agate Nesaule (formerly Krouse), Audrey Roberts, Ruth Schauer, Star Olderman, and Barbara G. Taylor.

39. Ellen Langill interviews with Agate Nesaule and Ruth Schauer.

40. *Final Report of the System Task Force on Women's Studies*; Ellen Langill interviews with Estella Lauter, Virginia Crane, and Barbara Sniffen.

41. Karen Merritt, "A Women's Studies Plan for Wisconsin," in Swoboda and Roberts, Vol. III, p. 53.

42. Personal communication, Helen Bannan to Laura Stempel Mumford.

43. Ellen Langill interviews with Estella Lauter and Sidney Bremer.

44. Ellen Langill interviews with Estella Lauter and Sidney Bremer.

45. Estella Lauter, "On Trying a Feminist's Soul," in Marian Swoboda, Audrey Roberts, and Jennifer Hirsch (eds.), *Women on Campus in the Eighties: Old Struggles, New Victories*, University Women: A Series of Essays (Madison: University of Wisconsin System Office of Women, 1993), Vol. IV, p. 64; Ellen Langill interviews with Estella Lauter, Sidney Bremer, and Julie Brickley.

46. Ellen Langill interview with Estella Lauter; personal communication, Estella Lauter to Laura Stempel Mumford, February 22, 1999.

47. Lauter, "On Trying a Feminist's Soul," p. 64.

48. Ellen Langill interview with Sidney Bremer.

Kathryn Clarenbach, 1972. (Photo courtesy of
University of Wisconsin–Madison Archives.)

Participants in the Wingspread Conference that kicked off the Soviet women's visit to the
UW System Women's Studies Consortium in October, 1991. Among those pictured are
Frances M. Kavenik, UW-Parkside (second from left) and Susan Stanford Friedman,
UW–Madison (fourth from left).

From left: Nedra Cobb (UW–Parkside), Ruth Schauer, Rebecca Hogan, Geneva Moore, Agate Nesaule, and Audrey Roberts (all from UW–Whitewater), at the UW System Women's Studies Consortium Fall Curriculum Mini-Conference, UW–Marinette, August, 1994.

Chapter 5

The Rise of a Statewide Women's Studies Network, 1974–1989

B y 1973, women's studies courses were being offered on half a dozen campuses of the University of Wisconsin System, and feminist activism was growing. The Regents had voted to investigate the establishment of interdisciplinary programs such as Afro-American Studies, and in 1973, Vice President for Academic Affairs Donald Smith paved the way for major change when he created a Systemwide Task Force on Women's Studies to examine the need and feasibility of developing women's studies programs on all of Wisconsin's campuses. The final report of this Task Force was a crucial turning point for faculty, staff members, and students committed to the new field, and gave them a powerful administrative sanction to push for additional courses and for the establishment of formal women's studies programs in every institution of the UW System.

Not surprisingly, membership on the Task Force immediately became controversial. Members of the Wisconsin Coordinating Council for Women in Higher Education (WCCWHE) petitioned Smith to have some input into the selection of members, as did members of UW-Madison's Association of Faculty Women (AFW). Others argued that appointing women already working within the UW administration—such as the already controversial Cyrena Pondrom—would lend the final report greater clout and a better chance for success. Smith yielded to several of the requests for women members from campuses around the System, but remained adamantly opposed to the request to select feminist activist and Educational Policy assistant professor Joan Roberts, believing her to be too radical and even disruptive.[1]

Despite this reluctance, though, Task Force members and staff included many women who had already emerged as key figures in feminist activism across Wisconsin. The project was staffed by Karen Merritt, Senior Academic Planner for the University of Wisconsin System, and a scholar already active in women's studies.[2] Members of the Task Force included Kay Clarenbach (UW-Extension), Joan Yeatman (UW-La Crosse), Cyrena Pondrom (UW-Madison), Marian Swoboda (UW System Office of Women), Lenore Harmon (UW-Milwaukee), and Chair Barbara Desmarais (now Taylor) (UW-Whitewater), as well as 12 other members from across the System. Nevertheless, WCCWHE members expressed disappointment that they had not been consulted about appointments to the group. In response, Smith described the "inclusive process" he envisioned that would allow them to preview a draft copy of the report and make suggestions, which would "give assurance that any deficiencies in the initial document which may be observed by the Coordinating Council will be fully aired before we consider the document as a finished product."[3]

The Task Force began to conduct public hearings and surveys, holding a series of public meetings and discussion forums throughout the University via the Educational Telephone Network (ETN) in order to be inclusive and generate widespread interest around the System. Task Force members also corresponded with a number of other universities about the structure of their women's studies programs, although (then as now) no other states had perfectly comparable unified university systems.[4]

When the preliminary draft of the report was completed early in 1974, the WCCWHE, among other groups, reviewed it and submitted a seven-page response, which endorsed the draft but made a number of significant recommendations, including the idea that women's studies be defined as "on, about, and *for* women." The WCCWHE also asked that the report strengthen its attention to the value of scholarly research on women: "The promotion for its own sake of scholarship in this long-neglected research field is fully as important and as deserving of mention as the suggestion that social betterment will result from the adoption of Women's Studies Programs."[5] The WCCWHE also suggested that an emphasis be placed on the creation of graduate-level as well as undergraduate programs, that the women's studies coordinators on each campus be full-time, and that the U.S. Department of Health, Education and Welfare (HEW) guidelines for the implementation of Title IX and its effects on women's studies be "publicized throughout the university system." The deadline for the submission of campus budgets for the 1975–77 state biennial budget was rapidly nearing and the WCCWHE feared that further delays would only slow the momentum built by the Task Force's work.[6]

The Task Force's final report, completed in September, described the new field as:

> a growing area of knowledge which should be recognized as integral to the curriculum and vital to the fulfillment of the Mission of the University. Women's Studies seeks not only to expand understanding of the female experience but also to examine the ways in which interpretations of human history have been altered or distorted by the traditional tendency to focus almost exclusively on the accomplishments and perceptions of men. By a systematic reexamination of human knowledge, Women's Studies will provide new approaches to the search for truth.[7]

In recommending that each UW institution establish a women's studies program, the report addressed the areas of curriculum, program structure, faculty, budget, and Systemwide resources. The Task Force urged each campus to develop an interdisciplinary major, minor, and/or certificate, new courses in the natural and social sciences, and graduate courses where appropriate, and recommended the establishment of a research center "with a Systemwide orientation."[8] In terms of administrative structure, the Task Force had concluded that creating women's studies *departments* might isolate their members' intellectual endeavors, whereas a *program* that crossed many disciplines would allow courses about women to remain an integral part of the mainstream curriculum.

The funding and responsibilities of a program coordinator—a "monumental" task[9]—were described in some detail, and the report recommended that the coordinator's position be full-time, "and in no instances should it be less than a half-time position,"[10] a goal that has, even 25 years later, been achieved on only a few of the UW System campuses. The continuing importance of outreach, community involvement, and a public service component for each program was also emphasized, and funding was urged for new faculty hires, research leaves, additional library and other resource materials, and the development of a position for a Systemwide librarian or bibliographer whose office could act as both a clearinghouse for information and as a resource for scholarly research. This last idea was later delegated to a special committee, and in 1977, the position of UW System Women's Studies Librarian-at-Large was established (described later in this chapter).

At campuses throughout the UW System, the report of the 1974 Task Force provided new energy for women's studies program and curriculum development, and many program coordinators, both at the time and recalling it years later, called it a watershed for women's studies in Wisconsin's state colleges and universities. Amidst the continued frustrations over HEW compliance and affirmative action plans that seemed to exist only on paper, the Regents' acceptance of the full report was significant and empowering. Because they could now argue that the Regents themselves had mandated change, the report provided the official imprimatur for women across the System to demand the expansion of women's studies programs.[11]

As a direct result of this, most of the four-year campuses would develop more complete curricula, programs, and in some cases even women's studies minors over the next five years. Although its full acceptance as a rigorous discipline was still years away—and in some cases has not happened even now—women's studies sought to enter the academic mainstream. With its emphasis on research, the Regents' approval also set the stage for the establishment of a research center that would provide funding for scholarship, although it would take several years for such a center to be created, and when it was, it did not follow the statewide model the Task Force had proposed.

By 1978, as Chapter 6 will show, women's studies programs had been established in most institutions, but budgetary support was often merely token, and staff, faculty, and administrators faced a new set of problems. Especially overburdened were the administrators: With only quarter- to eighth-time releases and heavy teaching overloads, most of them were actually volunteering more hours to their campuses than they had ever done. Affirmative action goals were also not being met, and the gains in hiring, retaining, and tenuring women faculty had fallen far behind the 1971 hopes of the founders of the WCCWHE. In the seven years since the group's establishment, the number of women faculty Systemwide had increased less than two percent, and many other issues concerning promotion, salary equity, and the status of academic and classified staff also remained unresolved. As one founding member of the WCCWHE wrote, "The position paper presented to [System] Vice President Donald Smith in June of 1978 shows how much of the early agenda remained to be accomplished."[12]

During this period, however, with formal programs expanding around the System, the WCCWHE gradually began to be superseded by a network of women's studies coordinators, whom System planner Karen Merritt (and later, her successor, Cara Chell) convened at semi-annual meetings. These meetings dealt with a wide variety of issues at both the campus and state level, from curricular changes, proposals for women's studies minors or majors, and local political conflicts to the planning of statewide conferences and Wisconsin's representation in regional and national organizations.

As the years went on, the group also provided an opportunity for administrators to work on joint projects—such as the development of an audio-visual collection—and to collaborate on the grant proposals that would eventually lead to the establishment of a formal statewide organization, the Women's Studies Consortium (described in Chapter 8). The 1977 opening of the first statewide women's studies office—the Women's Studies Librarian-at-Large—also helped to unite women's studies practitioners around Wisconsin, and the organization of annual statewide conferences (which continues to this day) provided regular opportunities for scholars, teachers, and students to meet and exchange ideas about research and the rapidly expanding women's studies curriculum.

WCCWHE members regretted the demise of an organization that had meant so much to them and had accomplished so much for women throughout the UW System. Jackie Macaulay wondered whether the statewide movement the group had represented had become moribund out of apathy, discouragement, or complete despair. "When academic women in particular see their efforts constantly frustrated, see repeated failures to bring about significant changes in their institutions, see that cutbacks and layoffs throughout education are rapidly taking away the little we have so laboriously gained, at such heavy personal cost, many of us are losing heart."[13] Others suggested that the early energy and momentum that had gone into the creation and maintenance of the WCCWHE had now been siphoned off into the campus women's studies programs and the tremendous amount of time demanded to maintain them. Perhaps, also, the 1974 Task Force, which had focused on women's studies, had shifted attention from the broader issues of women's status as employees and students. Whatever the causes, the WCCWHE as a formal group ceased to exist in the spring of 1979, even after several members tried to maintain it solely as a telephone committee. One optimistic observer argued that perhaps the WCCWHE had died of its own success.

As an ongoing link among campus women for the next decade—until the 1989 creation of the Systemwide Women's Studies Consortium—the coordinators' group brought together the administrators of women's studies programs from all of the System's campuses to exchange ideas, share frustrations, and shape new goals. The coordinators' spring business meetings filled the communication gap left by the demise of the WCCWHE, and helped to keep the programs and leaders on each campus from being completely isolated. However, the end of the WCCWHE, the first statewide organization in which women across the University of Wisconsin System organized on their own behalf, marked the end of an important era.

In 1980, the UW System sponsored a new Task Force, this one specifically established to investigate the status of women. While the group's 1981 report made recommendations on a wide range of employment, safety, and student-oriented issues, it also reinforced the 1974 Task Force's recommendation that each campus within the System establish a women's studies program and sustain it despite funding declines or budget cuts. By 1983, only the Centers and UW-River Falls were unable to meet this requirement.[14]

A special one-day symposium was also held in the spring of 1981 in Madison, co-sponsored by the UW Center System and the UW-Madison Women's Studies Program. Its goal was to encourage faculty at the two-year UW Centers and on several four-year campuses to offer courses in their disciplines that could be cross-listed with Women's Studies, and it was followed by a three-week seminar in late May and early June, at which the participants were given the background needed to design interdisciplinary courses and to "integrat[e] women's studies content and methodology into courses in primarily humanistic disciplines." The seminar focused on three areas: an introduction to the field of women's studies and to major concepts and issues in feminist theory; an examination of the ways in which cultural paradigms had structured notions of sexual difference; and an exploration of curriculum, pedagogy, and methodology for women's studies classrooms.[15] It ended with the assignment of mentors from the UW-Madison program to work with seminar participants in their own disciplines on the implementation and design of new women's studies courses for the 1981–82 academic year.

At a follow-up gathering in the spring of 1982, participants discussed the success of the new courses and the problems they had encountered. The report was mixed. Many participants were enthusiastic after leaving the seminar and began to integrate feminist concepts and theory into new and existing courses. However, at the Center campuses, resistance to cross-listing courses continued, as did a lack of time and local resources, and participants had trouble connecting with a mentor in their precise academic field. Nevertheless, the project gave a boost to the development of women's studies courses and provided a valuable link both among the participants themselves and between them and their mentors in Madison.[16]

* * * * *

Before the 1974 Task Force on Women's Studies had completed its work, a sub-committee of the Madison-based Association of Faculty Women (AFW) had proposed the creation of a position for a Systemwide women's studies librarian, and those recommendations had been included in the appendix to the Task Force's final report.[17] Although the proposal to include such a position in the System's biennial budget for 1975–77 failed (in fact, no new programs of any kind were funded in that budget), the work of the committee continued, with a new goal of establishing a librarian's office by 1977.[18]

The development of women's studies programs at campuses across the System and the explosion of feminist research and curriculum transformation across the country made the need for the Librarian-at-Large position even more immediate than it had been. It was rapidly becoming difficult for individual faculty members and researchers to keep track of everything going on in the new field, and it was clear that a librarian would be invaluable in finding the resources and materials to develop new courses and improve existing ones, encouraging faculty research, and serving as a curricular clearinghouse that could distribute not only scholarly and other information from outside sources, but even course syllabi from within and outside of the UW System.

To highlight the importance of the proposed position, proponents held a conference in the spring of 1976 entitled "The Development of Resources for Women's Studies." One of the greatest needs, according to conference participants, was for a central bibliography, a list of women's studies resource materials at all of Wisconsin's campuses, which could be made available through the Wisconsin Interlibrary Loan Service (WILS). Based on this and other conference proposals, UW System Vice President Donald Smith recommended that the position of Women's Studies Librarian be funded by the System and suggested a two-year pilot from 1977 to 1979.[19] With this funding approved, the University of Wisconsin thus became the first—and still the only—university in the country to fund a central Systemwide Women's Studies Librarian.

With the salary and travel expenses for a Women's Studies Librarian (WSL) now underwritten for two years, the next question was where the office would be housed. Nancy Marshall, Director of WILS, offered to provide space in the WILS office at the UW-Madison's main Memorial Library, thus giving the position the support of library resources there, connecting it to the interlibrary loan service, and also offering a staffing home for supervisory purposes. Direct supervisory responsibility for the Women's Studies Librarian's office was to be under the control of a separate Advisory Panel, and a search to fill the new position resulted in the selection of a graduate of the University of Chicago Library School, Esther Stineman (later Lanigan), who began her job in September, 1977.

During the three years of her tenure as Women's Studies Librarian, Stineman served as an important conduit of information and support for women's studies faculty and staff at all of the UW System campuses. She visited each campus, attended the coordinators' twice-yearly meetings, and received a grant from the Undergraduate Teaching Improvement Council (UTIC)—a System office supporting innovations and faculty development in undergraduate teaching—to develop an audiotape/slide presentation, which highlighted the need for curriculum and resource development and the importance of research on women in the social sciences, humanities, and history.[20] She also put together the first general resource text in women's studies in the country, *Women's Studies: A Recommended Core List*, published in 1979 and hailed by pioneer feminist publisher Florence Howe as "the single most useful reference tool in women's studies published thus far."[21]

The two-year pilot funding for the WSL position was renewed in 1979, with the additional support of two part-time assistants, but Stineman decided to return to graduate school that same year and was replaced by Linda Parker, a librarian and women's studies specialist at the University of Kansas at Lawrence. Parker increased her office's visibility with her many journeys across the state, and also made the office into a clearinghouse for news from each program in Wisconsin and from women's studies programs across the country. She helped to bring new computer technologies to women's studies research by launching a national effort to develop an electronic database in women's studies, by the National Council for Research on Women (NCRW).[22]

Parker also compiled newsletters and publications that included lists of new periodicals, books, and articles in the field of women's studies, and these publications soon reached a wide audience around the country, with subscriptions provided free of charge to librarians eager to develop women's studies resources, as well as to teachers in universities and on the secondary level. Like Stineman's work in setting up the office in its first two years, Parker's work helped to establish the University of Wisconsin as a leading resource for materials development and extended the services of Wisconsin's unique Women's Studies Librarian position to borders beyond the state, throughout the country, and even overseas.[23]

Writing for the *Women's Studies Newsletter* about the importance of the work of the Women's Studies Librarian in 1980, Parker coined her version of a feminist librarians' motto: "building networks, disseminating new information and research, launching new campaigns for change, stirring new insights, and nurturing our growth as individuals." She saw change coming to many universities through the work of feminist librarians who were "challenging institutional policies and practices which form barriers to both women workers and women library users." Activist librarians, such as Wisconsin's WSL, were crucial to the development of women's studies programs, as well as to the growth of awareness within their larger communities.[24]

Before her departure in 1981, Parker had begun three important publications, all initially offered free of charge: *Feminist Collections: Women's Studies Library Resources in Wisconsin*; *New Books on Women and Feminism*; and *Feminist Periodicals: A Current Listing of Contents*. She also completed the directory *Women's Studies in Wisconsin: Who's Who and Where*, first published in September, 1980. Royalty fees from the publication of the Stineman bibliography were used in 1981 to purchase the office's first desktop computer.[25]

The path was not always smooth, however, and Parker realized that she often had to tread carefully because of budget-tightening problems and censorship issues. She recognized that at some campuses her presence brought clout to the local women's studies committee or provided them with an occasion to schedule a much-delayed meeting with administrators. Sometimes, in fact, she was the only person from the UW System who was able to visit women's studies faculty and offer advice and encouragement. She also helped acquisitions librarians defend their choices for collection development, particularly in the face of battles with local campus committees trying to censor acquisitions of women's studies materials because of their controversial content, and she met with deans and library supervisors around the state to underscore the importance of staying abreast of the new field. As a Southerner, one of her greatest problems involved all of the winter driving, and the many overnight stays as she traveled from one corner of the state to the other made her realize first-hand what the implications of the Wisconsin Idea—that "the borders of the university are the borders of the state"—really were.[26]

Oversight of Parker's position remained in the hands of the Advisory Panel, a group that also served as a support network for her. Additional stability for the WSL position came in the summer of 1980, when it was permanently transferred as a staff line to UW-Madison, although System funding still underwrote the salary. During her tenure as WSL, Parker learned a lot about the complex politics of aligning staffing and budget requests in a large university system, and she became adept at getting funding for new services. On one campus visit, Parker recalled being teased by a Dean with the stock phrase, "you don't look like a feminist!" After the Dean apologized for the remark, Parker persuaded him to commit to providing funding from his budget for a full-time assistant to support her WSL position, but even with his promise of funding in hand, Parker still had to get approval for the salary line itself. She hastened back to Madison to meet with System Planner Karen Merritt, who helped to secure the necessary approval for a new line. Although this new full-time assistant/editor line was actually occupied by two half-time employees, the additional staffing not only improved such basic office functions as record-keeping, but also greatly increased Parker's freedom to travel to campuses around the state.[27]

However, in 1981, just one year after the WSL position was taken off of pilot status and made permanent, Parker decided to leave the position for an administrative library position at another university. The next Women's Studies Librarian-at-

Large was Sue Searing, who was determined to build upon her predecessors' successes in both publications and campus ambassadorship for women's studies.

On her visits around the state, Searing kept a journal that described the status of women's studies programs and the types of issues she discussed with campus personnel. She was determined that the administrators on each campus come to recognize the importance and legitimacy of women's studies and to realize that it represented "an intellectual sea change."[28] While Searing's visits provided support to local women's studies faculty and staff, that relationship was also reciprocal, for in setting up these visits, Searing found that her Advisory Panel could often smooth the way and help her establish at least one liaison with each campus in the System.

What really stood out, and surprised me at the time, was how much fuss people made when I visited. The Librarian-at-Large position had "Madison" and "System" radiating from it like an aura. I was escorted to meetings with chancellors, vice chancellors, and deans, as well as library directors and women's studies faculty. Sometimes I was asked to make a formal presentation, but often my role was to show up and demonstrate by my presence that System Administration supported women's studies. I'm not sure that I really impressed the bigwigs, but I know I boosted the morale of the leaders of struggling women's studies programs. And on many campuses, the librarians were a good source of support, too. After all, in a female-intensive profession, there's bound to be a certain percentage of feminists. Among the librarians, I rarely had to convince anyone to acquire women's studies books and journals. Rather, our office aided by consolidating bibliographic references, publishing reviews, and giving advice and tools to help the libraries fulfill their mission of supporting an emerging curriculum.

At UW-Oshkosh, Barbara Sniffen was heading the women's studies program. When I arrived on campus, I discovered that, in addition to the usual round of meetings, I was going to be a guest on her radio show on the campus station. Not just a casual interview, but the focus of the entire hour! Library issues can't hold an audience's attention for that long, so our conversation ranged far and wide. I remember expounding opinions about teen pregnancy, welfare, and who knows what else.

At another campus (I've forgotten which one, thankfully), the library director asked me what I'd be doing when I finished the women's studies project. I looked at him blankly. Oh, he insisted, the whole point of my position was to get libraries up to speed on women's studies, and then move on to other new fields. He was genuinely upset that this hadn't been made clear to me when I was hired.

He said that the UW's library directors would never have agreed to such a position if women's studies were to be its sole focus. I never encountered this attitude among the other library directors, so I can only conclude (as Karen Merritt assured me) that he had misunderstood.

—Sue Searing

Under Searing's leadership as the third WSL, inter-campus communication among women faculty regarding women's studies resources was heightened, publications supporting curricular and collection development were enhanced, and the position of women's studies as a valuable part of the interdisciplinary programs on Wisconsin campuses was solidified. The influence of her office also helped to develop the research potential of women's studies scholars who came to Wisconsin to teach, to write, or to share their works. A major achievement during Searing's nine-year tenure built upon Esther Stineman's earlier work. Together with Catherine Loeb and Stineman (then at Yale University), Searing compiled the second volume of *Women's Studies: A Recommended Core Bibliography 1980–1985*, published in 1987 and underwritten by the National Endowment for the Humanities. New and influential bibliographies on science and technology, race and ethnicity, and topical reading lists on other subjects also greatly expanded the office's contribution to women's studies research and teaching.[29]

Looking back on her years as Women's Studies Librarian, Searing credited the administration at Memorial Library for its willingness to pick up occasional budget shortfalls. "They were proud of the international reputation that Wisconsin had achieved with its first Systemwide Women's Studies Librarian position."[30] Additional evidence that library administrators recognized the importance of those resources came in 1987, when Searing took over the responsibility for women's studies collection development at Memorial Library, a separate activity that involved acquisitions beyond the WSL office.[31]

Notes

1. Letter from Adolph Y. Wilburn, Associate Vice President, Academic Affairs, to "All Chancellors and Vice Chancellors," October 10, 1973, in University Archives; letter from Donald K. Smith to "All Chancellors," September 19, 1973, in University Archives; Ellen Langill interviews with Jacqueline Macaulay and Donald K. Smith.

2. Merritt had been actively involved in the women's movement in Madison as a member of AFW and had been hired in the fall of 1970 to research the issue of salary inequity at the university in the Office of Analytical Studies. She had also contributed a lecture on the history of women in higher education for Joan Roberts' course.

3. Donald K. Smith, Letter to Mary Jo Buggs, Coordinator of the Wisconsin Coordinating Council on Women in Higher Education, March 15, 1974, University Archives.

4. Ellen Langill interview with Barbara G. Taylor (formerly Desmarais).

5. Leticia M. Smith (Chair), Edith M. Bjorklund, Agate N. Krouse, Jacqueline Macaulay, Jacqueline Ross (for the WCCWHE), "Response to the *Final Report* of the UW System Task Force on Women's Studies," July 1974.

6. Smith et al., "Response to Task Force."

7. *Final Report of the System Task Force on Women's Studies*, September 30, 1974, p. 1.

8. *Final Report of the System Task Force on Women's Studies*, pp. 2–3.

9. *Final Report of the System Task Force on Women's Studies*, p. 4.

10. *Final Report of the System Task Force on Women's Studies*, p. 6.

11. Ellen Langill interviews with Ruth Schauer, Agate Nesaule (formerly Krouse), Barbara Sniffen, and Estella Lauter.

12. Jacqueline Macaulay, "A History of the Coordinating Council of Women in Higher Education: The Boundaries for University Women Are the Boundaries of the State," in Marian Swoboda and Audrey Roberts (eds.), *Women Emerge in the Seventies*, University Women: A Series of Essays (Madison: University of Wisconsin System Office of Women, 1980), Vol. III, p. 33.

13. Macaulay, "A History," p. 31.

14. "A Blueprint for Achievement of Educational Equality in the Eighties: A Report of the Regents' Task Force on the Status of Women," April 1981.

15. "Final Report, Women's Studies Project."

16. "Final Report, Women's Studies Project."

17. Members of this committee included a number of women librarians and library administrators, among them Miriam Allman, Acquisitions Librarian, Medical

Library, UW-Madison; Edith Bjorklund, Acquisitions Librarian, UW-Milwaukee; Gretchen Lagana, Assistant to the Director, Memorial Library, UW-Madison; Nancy Marshall, Director, Wisconsin Interlibrary Loan Service; and Dorothy Schultz, Director, College Library, UW-Madison.

18. Sue Searing, "Women's Studies Librarian," in Marian Swoboda, Audrey Roberts, and Jennifer Hirsch (eds.), *Women on Campus in the Eighties: Old Struggles, New Victories*, University Women: A Series of Essays (Madison: University of Wisconsin System Office of Women, 1993), Vol. IV, pp. 35–41.

19. Phyllis Holman Weisbard, "University of Wisconsin System Office of the Women's Studies Librarian: Program Review/Self-Study," July 19, 1993; Searing, "Women's Studies Librarian," p. 35.

20. Ellen Langill interview with Esther (Stineman) Lanigan; Searing, "Women's Studies Librarian," p. 37.

21. Quoted in Weisbard, "Program Review," p. iv.

22. Searing, "Women's Studies Librarian," p. 38.

23. Ellen Langill interviews with Linda Parker and Phyllis Holman Weisbard.

24. Linda Parker, "HQ 1100–HQ 1870—A Librarian's View of the Second NWSA Convention," in *Women's Studies Newsletter*, Vol. VIII, No. 3, Summer 1980, p. 10.

25. Ellen Langill interview with Linda Parker.

26. Ellen Langill interview with Linda Parker; Parker, "HQ 1100."

27. Ellen Langill interview with Linda Parker; Parker, "HQ 1100."

28. Ellen Langill interview with Sue Searing.

29. Ellen Langill interview with Sue Searing; Searing, "Women's Studies Librarian," p. 38.

30. Ellen Langill interview with Sue Searing.

31. Searing, "Women's Studies Librarian," p. 40.

Chapter 6

The Women's Studies Program at the University of Wisconsin-Madison

Although a variety of women's studies courses had been developed on the University of Wisconsin-Madison campus by the fall of 1974, there still remained the task of creating a coherent program. In response to the 1974 report from the UW System Task Force on Women's Studies, Madison Chancellor Edwin Young created a Committee on Women's Studies charged with "evaluating campus needs and resources in the area of Women's Studies and bringing forward recommendations concerning campus actions to meet those needs."

Co-chaired by Elizabeth Fennema, a faculty member in the School of Education's Department of Curriculum and Instruction, and Jane Piliavin (then in Child and Family Studies), committee appointees also included long-time feminist activist and teacher Annis Pratt (English), as well as Barbara Bitters, who had taught "Alice in Academe" as a graduate student. The committee's staff included Susan Stanford Friedman, who had received her Ph.D. in English in 1973 and had just returned to Madison from teaching at Brooklyn College. Once again, as with the Task Force itself and other important appointments in women's studies history, the committee's membership became a volatile issue.[1] Fennema and Piliavin recognized that they had been selected in part because they were tenured and because they were viewed as "non-aligned" moderates, and others believed that the very process by which appointments were made was a deliberately devious one. Annis Pratt recalls that administrators chose "the summer [of 1974], when they thought we activists would all be away, to pack the committee with their allies," but in response, Pratt and Jacqueline Macaulay "devised a counter-strategy: a rota to make sure that one of us was in town at all times. . . . This way, we won our fight for a balanced committee."[2]

As had happened with earlier key appointments, members of the Association of Faculty Women (AFW) resented being left out of the selection process, and asked Young to appoint Ruth Bleier—not only a dedicated feminist activist, but also a tenured professor and a nationally known scientist—to the committee, but Young rejected the idea, despite the risk that the opposition of the only active faculty women's group on campus might actually interfere with the committee's progress. The AFW wanted a member of their core leadership to be on the committee, and took Young's refusal as a slap in the face.[3] However, a last-minute compromise was reached when Young accepted a new member, whom the women trusted: Diane Kravetz, then an untenured assistant professor in the School of Social Work, who was chosen one day and joined the committee the next.[4]

Much like its Systemwide predecessor, the UW-Madison committee held public hearings and quickly narrowed its focus to three overriding concerns: the structure of women's studies as part of the campus curriculum, the impact of women's studies research, and its outreach mission. The committee spent a great deal of time discussing the administrative and governance structures (a matter of national debate) and decided that creating a program that could cross all disciplines and departments was wiser than establishing women's studies as a department, where it could become marginalized and ignored. While a program could be granted the power to offer courses on its own, its teaching faculty would retain at least a 50% position in their home departments and be tenured there, making it impossible to eliminate them completely if support for women's studies disappeared.[5]

This decision was motivated not simply by the desire to make the program secure and stable, but also by the hope that in bringing faculty together from many fields, the program would become truly interdisciplinary. The committee also believed that intellectual respect for the emerging field would be well served if its teaching faculty had published scholarly research and received tenure in their own disciplines. The committee recommended housing the program in the College of Letters and Sciences (L&S), believing that women's studies fit well into the mission of liberal arts to question existing knowledge and seek new theoretical analyses. The program would have its own curricular number and its courses would have a spot in the campus Timetable listings.[6]

While the committee's attention was focused on these administrative issues, curriculum development was also underway—in one case actually getting ahead of the program-approval process. In the spring of 1975, Susan Friedman helped to design a new "Introduction to Women's Studies" course, and this was formally approved before the final report of the committee was submitted. (At the suggestion of the campus Divisional Committee that had to grant approval, the introductory course was divided into two separate courses, one devoted to work in the humanities, the other to the social sciences.[7]) As a result, the UW-Madison Faculty Senate—the governance group that had to vote on the committee's proposal to establish a women's studies program—was faced with having two courses approved before the program that would house them was officially created.[8]

In May 1975, the program was approved by the Faculty Senate, and L&S Dean David Cronon became responsible for making it a reality by the Fall semester. He followed the committee's recommendations that its chair, Jane Piliavin, be asked to serve as the first program chair, but she turned him down, and when he called a second time, she submitted a list of essentials that she believed he could not fulfill. When Cronon put the package together in less than 24 hours, Piliavin accepted the new position.[9]

Piliavin's demands helped to shape the course of the Women's Studies Program's development for many years to come. Because she requested a building of their own, Cronon found a campus house on Brooks Street just one block south of the main campus, with space for offices and meetings. The program was staffed with a full-time program assistant, and Piliavin was allowed to hire three faculty members with joint appointments in the first year and got a permanent budget line that included expenses to run the program. Susan Friedman became the program's first Associate Chair, and its first Executive Committee included several members from the Task Force that had helped to design the program's structure.[10]

The proposal for the Women's Studies Program had included a carefully designed governance structure that lasted for the program's first sixteen years. In accordance with the policies and procedures of the University, the ballots of the Executive Committee (officially consisting only of tenured faculty members) were formally recorded on matters of personnel and budget, but in practice, all program members—including staff, students, untenured faculty, and members of the Madison community—had a vote on these and all other matters, and the Executive Committee made its recommendation to the dean based on the vote of the whole.[11] An attempt was always made to reach decisions by consensus, which was considered a more egalitarian governance method than strict majority rule, although difficult questions were sometimes resolved by majority vote.

During the next few years, members shaped the new program through intense debates at weekly meetings. (On one memorable occasion late in the 1970s, there was a long and heated session over the issue of remodeling the kitchen in the house, when a faculty member objected "vociferously" to the removal of the kitchen sink, which had been requested by the program assistant who used that room as her office.[12]) Other discussions were equally passionate, as program members debated issues of sexual orientation, the development of courses in lesbian studies, the needs of women of color, and whether male faculty should be allowed to teach in women's studies—topics that aroused controversy for women's studies practitioners and other feminists throughout Wisconsin and around the country.[13] That intensity continued as the program grew, and the monthly meetings of the 1980s drew crowds so large that the living room at Brooks Street was often filled to overflowing.

Over the next ten years, the UW-Madison Women's Studies Program experienced tremendous growth in the number of its faculty and the breadth of its curricular offerings, and achieved national prominence for the scholarly contribution of its members. In celebration of the decade since the report of the 1974 UW System Task Force that had recommended the establishment of formal programs like Madison's, the program sponsored a conference in the fall of 1984, featuring research papers on developments in women's studies in a variety of fields, from the humanities and sciences to music and architecture, and talks on topics such as "Integrating Women's Studies in the Curriculum." The keynote address came from Barbara Taylor (formerly Desmarais), then at the University of Arkansas, who had chaired the System Task Force.[14] By the next year, when the UW-Madison program celebrated its own tenth birthday, its faculty included members of 22 different departments, representing the colleges of Letters and Science, Medicine,

Nursing, Education, Family Resources and Consumer Sciences, Agricultural and Life Sciences, and Extension. Even as program members celebrated, recounting the often turbulent history of this first decade, they were working to expand their ability to serve students: a proposal to establish a major was under consideration by the Regents, who approved it in October.[15]

By 1986, the UW-Madison Women's Studies Program had 23 permanent courses on the books, along with four directed studies courses. Counting those enrolled in cross-listed courses, more than 2,000 students took women's studies courses each year. Undergraduates could elect a 15-credit certificate or a 30-credit major—20 students declared a major in its first semester, Fall 1986—and graduate students could choose between two options for a graduate minor.[16]

The program had eight jointly-appointed faculty, ten teaching assistants, and a number of lecturers hired to teach specific courses. Ruth Bleier—one of the founders of the AFW, the Wisconsin Coordinating Council of Women in Higher Education (WCCWHE), and the Women's Studies Program itself—was completing four years as Chair, to be succeeded by Virginia Sapiro, one of the first four faculty hired by the new program in 1976, with a joint appointment in political science.[17]

The UW-Madison Women's Studies Program enjoyed the strongest budgetary support of any within the System, with 50% positions for the program Chair and the Director of the Women's Studies Research Center (described below), a 25%-time Associate Chair, two full-time classified staff members,[18] and eight joint faculty appointments and a 1986 base budget of $170,000. The tremendous gap between program size and budget on the two bigger campuses (the UW-Milwaukee's Center for Women's Studies had a budget of approximately $100,000) and in the remaining four-year and two-year institutions—where women's studies often got only $1,000 to $3,000 a year for all expenses—often led to misunderstandings over the relative burdens and responsibilities borne by the various programs. Administrators of the smaller programs often felt that the UW-Madison program members in particular did not really want to be involved in Systemwide meetings and conferences, and resentment sparked emotional exchanges at the semiannual coordinators' meetings, despite Madison administrators' efforts to "tread very carefully even while being attacked."[19]

But soon after Sapiro became Chair, Systemwide budget cuts were instituted, and like units across the University, the program suffered a base-budget cut in 1986, and feared worse to come: "The question," Sapiro wrote, "is how much will we be cut, and what will Women's Studies share be."[20] However, by 1988 some of the worst fears of budget cuts had not been realized and the UW-Madison program continued to expand. By the fall of 1988, there were more than 70 majors, and UW-Madison professor of women's history Gerda Lerner (who had helped pioneer the field of women's studies at Sarah Lawrence College in the late 1960s) called the program "probably the best women's studies program in the U.S."[21]

Sadly, though, despite these achievements, the program was soon to endure several difficult transitions. On January 4, 1988, Ruth Bleier died of cancer. From her earliest years in medicine at Johns Hopkins University and as professor of Neurophysiology at UW-Madison, Bleier had served as a mentor for women and as a key figure in the development of feminist activism on the Madison campus and a founder of the Women's Studies Program. Bleier's 1984 book, *Science and Gender: A Critique of Biology and Its Theories on Women*, was a pathbreaking study, and as one of the few women scientists to remain active in laboratory research while also pursuing a theoretical critique of science, her national contribution was unique and influential.

Bleier's abilities as a leader, a peacemaker, and her national reputation as a scholar blended with her unfailing energy and willingness to speak at campuses around the state on women's issues and her own research on gender and biology. When Bleier's two children, many close friends, colleagues, and admirers gathered for a memorial service, UW-Madison's new Chancellor Donna Shalala praised her contributions to women's studies, feminist scholarship, and the improvements in women's status throughout the University. Soon after her death, the Women's Studies Program established the annual Ruth Bleier Scholarship for Women in the Natural Sciences, in honor of the woman Program Chair Virginia Sapiro saluted as "one of the people who is most responsible for the women's studies [program] existing. She defined its direction and style."[22]

Ruth [Bleier] was unique among scientists who are feminists in that she did not leave her feminism at the laboratory door. She spent hours explaining the connections between feminism and science to her colleagues and friends who were not scientists. She used her feminist analysis to critique existing theories of science, to point out racist and sexist flaws in experimental design and interpretation, and to begin to sketch the parameters for feminist science. . . .

Ruth was also unusual among feminists in that she continued to be a practicing scientist while working on and writing about feminism and science and during the four years that she chaired the Women's Studies Program. The small group of feminists [around the country] interested in questions of science and feminism consists primarily of historians and philosophers of science. Fewer members of the group have Ph.D.s and teach in traditional scientific disciplines. Of those who do, most . . . have changed their research focus towards feminism and science, gradually dropping . . . "hard science," grant-supported research along the way. Ruth, however, continued active neuroanatomy research, well-supported by federal grants, while also writing on feminism and science. In fact, her best known

> *single-authored book, Science and Gender, and a monograph on the cat brain were published simultaneously in 1984.*
>
> *Ruth was a feminist scientist who could most skillfully use the methods and theories of feminism to critique science and the tools of science to analyze flaws in the methodology and theoretical constructs of feminism. She was unique in that respect. With her death on January 4, 1988, the world lost a scientist, a feminist, a feminist scientist, and a friend.*
>
> *—Sue Rosser[23]*

* * * * *

After Ruth Bleier died, the UW-Madison Women's Studies Program faced a crisis over its governance structure. From the program's earliest days, it had operated through an unusually open system of participation. Rather than making personnel and certain other decisions exclusively through an Executive Committee of tenured faculty members, as University regulations required, the program held "open" and "closed" meetings. Membership in the so-called "open" meeting consisted of all active participants in the program, including faculty of all ranks, graduate and undergraduate students, lecturers, classified staff, teaching assistants, and community members. The "closed" meeting included all program members who had attended meetings and done committee work for at least a year, and the Executive Committee endorsed its decisions and formally relayed them to University administration or (in the case of support for hiring, promotion, and tenure) to other departments. In addition, the program had three standing committees: Curriculum, which dealt with the development of new courses and other aspects of the program's curriculum; Personnel, which handled hiring and other personnel issues; and Research, essentially the advisory board for the Women's Studies Research Center. Membership on the Curriculum and Research Committees followed the "open" meeting rules; Personnel Committee members had to be members of the "closed" meeting.[24]

During Virginia Sapiro's tenure as Chair in the late 1980s, a rising tide of anger and frustration led to what some people saw as increasing hostility at program meetings.[25] The program had already weathered many conflicts over the same issues—racial and ethnic diversity, sexuality, identity politics, definitions of feminism—that had divided both feminists and women's studies practitioners throughout the country; but by 1990, questions of governance became a source of new friction.[26] During the late 1980s, women on many other campuses were undergoing the same bitter disillusionment with the organized women's movement and with academic feminists, and many believed that established feminists involved in women's studies had been co-opted by the University.[27] For Sapiro, some relief from the increasing tension at home came from the annual Women's Studies Directors' meetings of the Committee on Institutional Cooperation (CIC), the academic arm of the Big Ten Athletic Conference, where she found that the tensions appeared much the same in most programs.[28] Ironically, however, while some women's studies programs faced a lack of attendance at program meetings, in Madison, the opposite extreme was the case.[29]

By the time Betsy Draine of the English department became Chair in 1989, many members of the Women's Studies faculty believed that the time had come to rethink program governance. Some of the pressure for restructuring came from junior faculty who were soon to come up for tenure, some of whom feared that such a wide-open, all-member personnel evaluation might impair their chances, and therefore pushed for conformity to the strict procedural guidelines of standard University governance.[30] An Ad Hoc Committee met during 1990 and early 1991 to redraw the governance plan, limiting the historically open voting to a new design that would conform to the University mandate that only tenured faculty be allowed to vote on personnel issues. Program members were invited to a "Town Meeting" to speak and make suggestions, but the final voting was accomplished through written ballots of two distinct colors, one for general members and one for Executive Committee members.[31] In the spring of 1991, after heated debate, the proposal was approved, although the new structure "grandmothered" in existing program members and set aside seats for undergraduate and graduate students, community members, and others, so that they could vote on the newly-constituted Program Committee.[32]

Opponents angrily denounced the move as hierarchical, anti-feminist, and elitist, because it eliminated several major constituencies from voting rights on program personnel and budget, specifically students, junior faculty, staff, and affiliated community members, although they could still be Program Committee members and could vote on curricular issues. Defenders of the restructuring, however, argued that the time had come to conform to University procedures in substance as well as form if the program was to be fully accepted and respected as an academic unit on campus.[33]

It was a very painful and bitter time in the history of the program, and although most members continued their affiliation, a number angrily renounced their membership in protest of what they perceived as exclusionary politics and a change from the feminist inclusiveness of the past. One letter from a graduate student renouncing her affiliation noted her "deep regret and keen sense of sadness" as she resigned "as a symbol of my protest against the direction this Women's Studies Program has taken." The writer, Leisa Meyer, characterized the restructuring as a "movement away from a vision of Women's Studies as a forum and space to challenge the structures, confines and elitism of academia," and viewed the new governance model as one "which embraces . . . rules and regulations which have made [the University] an unsafe place for so many, excluding those who have not accrued status . . . [where] those who founded this program [once] came together to create a space that would make the University a less painful and isolating place for women."[34]

The anger and pain at this perceived "sell-out" did not fade away, but instead left many wounds among some of the most ardently committed program members, who felt they no longer had a role. But, while restructuring cost the program some of its members, the core faculty continued their participation through teaching, research, and program governance.

Although she had been opposed to restructuring, as Chair from 1992 to 1998, Mariamne Whatley worked to implement it and to help the program "recover" from its aftermath.[35] She also continued to promote the program's ongoing commitment to women and science, which had begun with its first science course, "Biology and Psychology of Women." Whatley, who had originally come to the UW-Madison in 1977 as a postdoctoral fellow in plant pathology, had begun offering the course "Women and their Bodies in Health and Disease" the following fall. The course was enormously popular immediately, and was regularly enrolling 320 students each semester by the early 1980s. Taught since 1984 by Nancy Worcester, it continues to be one of the most popular on campus, enrolling 300 to 400 students each semester, but turning away three times that many.[36]

Whatley herself had moved from fellow to lecturer, then to budgeted faculty member with a joint appointment in Curriculum & Instruction, and finally to Associate Chair, before becoming Chair in 1992 (and Associate Dean of the School of Education in 1998). By 1992, the Women's Studies Program included 15 faculty members appointed jointly to the program, and members were rightfully proud that all of the program's budgeted joint faculty who came up for tenure were successful.[37] The program had increased its regular courses to eleven each semester, along with the cross-listed courses taught by additional faculty, and despite worries about further budget cuts for interdisciplinary programs, after a five-year trial, the women's studies major also received the Regents' final approval in 1992.[38]

Another key issue was space. The house at 209 N. Brooks Street was bursting with personnel, teaching assistants, and researchers, and had no more room for growth. Although the move took place after she left, in 1993, her final year as Chancellor of the UW-Madison, Donna Shalala—soon to become U.S. Secretary of Health & Human Services—decided that the Women's Studies Program and the Women's Studies Research Center (which had been founded in 1977) would be relocated to Commerce (later renamed Ingraham) Hall in the center of campus, where ample offices existed for staff, along with separate facilities for the Research Center.

Shalala recalled later that the first welcome she had received in the spring of 1988 when she arrived on campus as the new chancellor was a reception given for her by the Women's Studies program,[39] and throughout her time as Chancellor, Shalala—the first woman leader of a Big Ten school—continued to provide support for women's studies. Through her efforts, the Women's Studies Program received its first endowed chair position, the Evjue Bascom Chair in Women's Studies, a distinguished faculty appointment which was held first by Judith Walzer Leavitt (history of medicine) and then by Janet S. Hyde (psychology). Shalala's commitment to diversity, a major feature of her tenure as Chancellor, also resulted in the appointment of several women of color to the UW-Madison faculty.[40]

By the early 1990s, the Women's Studies Program administration included a half-time Chair, a quarter-time Associate Chair, a half-time Director for the Research Center, and a new 75% Outreach Coordinator (see below). In 1992, following the recommendation contained in the five-year review of the major, the program also created the 40% position of Advisor. Until now, the Associate Chair had, in addition to her other duties, been advising majors, who now numbered over 140, and the newly-hired advisor also worked on study-abroad options and undergraduate research possibilities.

After more than twenty years without the ability to grant tenure, the Women's Studies Program realized another goal in the spring of 1997 when it hired Dionne Espinoza in a joint appointment with Chicano Studies—the first faculty member to have her tenure home in Women's Studies. Many members had originally supported program rather than departmental status because of a specific strategic advantage: the security of faculty members' tenure in established departments that could not be abolished if support for women's studies disappeared. The fact that, after more than twenty years of existence, the program had finally become able to grant tenure suggested that at least some of the anxieties that had prompted that choice had been resolved.[41]

* * * * *

Curriculum development, governance, and faculty job security were not the only areas that received attention. As women's studies grew during the 1970s, there was an increasing national focus on the importance of research and publications that would both support the increase in knowledge about women in many disciplines and also provide better materials for course development. The existence of archival facilities in support of women's scholarship was not new in the 1970s. The Schlesinger Library on the History of Women in America at Radcliffe College was founded in 1943, followed by the Sophia Smith Collection at Smith College, but few scholars knew of their existence, or made use of their vast holdings. One librarian at Radcliffe recalled that even in the 1960s, "if anyone walked through the door, we had a celebration."[42]

After the first few years of concentration on women's studies program development, however, several universities and privately funded facilities began to receive grants to establish centers for the sponsorship of research on women, including those at Cornell University, the University of Michigan, Rutgers University, Wellesley College, and Stanford University.[43] By 1980, there were dozens, including the University of Arizona's Southwest Institute for Research on Women (SIROW); the Center for Continuing Education of Women at the University of California-Berkeley; the Center for Women Policy Studies in Washington, D.C.; the Institute for Education and Research on Women and Work at Cornell University; the Higher Education Research Institute in Los Angeles; centers at the CUNY Graduate School and Columbia University in New York, and the Women's Studies Research Center in Madison. While their budgets, structures, and influence varied widely, these institutions helped to legitimize new feminist inquiries into a variety of disciplines and to support the publication of new research in Women's Studies.[44]

In Wisconsin, both the AFW and the WCCWHE had urged the establishment of a research center that would provide funding for scholarly work in women's studies, and the recommendation had been included in the 1974 report of the System Task Force on Women's Studies. In 1976, the UW-Milwaukee wrote the first grant proposal for such a center, but the plan collapsed when the Chancellor failed to endorse and submit it with his campus's biennial budget.[45]

The UW-Madison Women's Studies Program had also established a Research Committee in 1976 to investigate the idea of having such a center on its campus, and this effort was far more successful than Milwaukee's. When it was created in the spring of 1977, the Women's Studies Research Center (WSRC) became part of the program, with a two-year grant of $30,000 from the UW-Madison's Hilldale Fund for a half-time director.[46] The goals of the Center were to provide "an environment in which faculty and students can discover, examine critically, preserve and transmit knowledge, wisdom and values that will help insure the survival of the present and future generations with improvement in the quality of life."[47]

Elaine Marks, professor of French and Italian and one of the scholars responsible for introducing French feminist writing to the U.S., became the Center's first director in October, 1977. Concerned that supporting the WSRC out of the Women's Studies Program budget would prove too draining, Marks attempted to get separate funding for the Center. A direct budget line for the Center director's salary came from the office of Madison Chancellor Irving Shain, but because this was not enough to cover its activities, the Center constantly had to seek outside grants to survive.[48]

In her six years as Director, Marks' managed to secure substantial funding, including more than $174,000 from the Ford Foundation for a three-year project, "An Interdisciplinary Approach to the Study of Motherhood." The project was spearheaded by Marjorie Klein, a psychologist and professor of psychiatry in the

Medical School and a Wellesley graduate who had served on the original committee that sought approval for the Research Center. In thinking about the WSRC's structure, Klein was influenced by her knowledge of the Wellesley Center for Research on Women, which had been founded in 1974 with a grant from the Carnegie Corporation. Compared to the small operating budget at UW-Madison, the Wellesley grants were enormous (that Center enjoyed an income of more than $1.6 million by the 1980–81 academic year), but as a model, it served to remind women's studies scholars that research grants were available and that foundations were looking for worthwhile programs to fund.[49]

Klein was later the recipient of a grant from the National Institute of Mental Health to study risk factors in depression among women over 50, for which she designated the Research Center as principal administrator.[50] During Marks' tenure as Director, the Center also instituted a program for Honorary Fellows, to provide a research home for women's studies scholars from around the System and those without an academic home who lived in the community. This position provided an official University affiliation, a desk, library access, and stationery from the Center, albeit with no funding.[51] By 1985, there were six Honorary Fellows, who reported on their research in weekly Friday–afternoon colloquia.

Aware of the continuing importance of reaching out to the community with programs and lectures, Marks turned to Connie Threinen and Marian Thompson, who had operated so many successful programs through UW-Extension's Women's Educational Resources. Together, they were able to plan and publicize many of the Center's scholarly programs and to entice community women onto the campus to take part in the ongoing intellectual excitement generated by the lectures.[52] To further the scholarly impact of its programs, the Center also began to publish a "Working Papers" series, which included articles by resident scholars, and offered workshops and staff assistance in writing grant proposals The Center's outreach efforts were meant to stimulate research activity and scholarly interest throughout the UW System, an important contribution during the middle and late 1970s, when programs on campuses across the state were still being established.[53]

In 1986, after a one-year term by Suzanne Pingree (Agricultural Journalism), Janet Shibley Hyde, a prominent feminist scholar of psychology from Denison University, became the Center's new Director, with a joint appointment in the UW-Madison psychology department. Under Hyde's leadership, the Research Center received several key grants, including a million dollar award from the National Institute of Mental Health for a four-year study of maternity leave. She also secured funding from the Johnson Foundation, Northwestern Mutual Life Insurance Company, and Wisconsin Bell for a national conference on parental leave, and like all of the WSRC Directors, remained active on the national level in women's studies research networking through the National Council for Research on Women, which met annually in New York.[54] The Center also continued to publish the "Working Papers" series, including several written by Madison faculty in 1987, celebrating the Research Center's tenth anniversary.[55]

But perhaps Hyde's greatest achievement, and certainly one that had the most wide-reaching impact on women's studies across the UW System, was a major Ford Foundation grant for a statewide curriculum-reform initiative called the Women of Color in the Curriculum (WOCC) Project. The WOCC project represented an important expression of the UW-Madison Women's Studies Program's commitment to questions of race and ethnicity, including the integration of the experiences and histories of women of color not only into women's studies courses, but into the program staff as well. Earlier efforts had included the establishment of program committees on anti-racism, specific courses on the intersections of race and gender, and activities such as speakouts.[56]

The WOCC project, which ran from 1989 to 1992, was actually a joint effort by the WSRC and the UW System Office of Multicultural Affairs and involved women's studies and other faculty, staff, and students from around the state. The initial Ford grant of $95,000 provided funding for curriculum-transformation activities at ten System campuses and in three UW-Madison departments, intended both to lead to the creation of new courses and to revise existing ones.[57] Activities included workshops and provided welcome support for curriculum-reform work that had been difficult for women's studies faculty to accomplish.

The grant came at a time when the UW System was becoming especially sensitive to the issue of racial and ethnic diversity. Two major UW initiatives—UW-Madison Chancellor Donna Shalala's "Madison Plan" and System President Kenneth Shaw's "Design for Diversity"—were aimed at increasing the diversity among faculty and students, and granting agencies like the Ford Foundation were becoming interested in statewide projects with the power to transform curriculum on a large number of public campuses at once. The Centers for Research on Women had been invited to propose projects like this one for a nationwide program that would integrate new scholarship on women of color into introductory and other courses within the liberal arts curriculum. As Beverly Guy-Sheftall, a nationally known scholar of Afro-American studies and a spokesperson for the Ford Foundation effort, noted, "the goal is to reconceptualize women's studies. To have it be more global—women don't have a monolithic experience."[58]

Cyrena Pondrom succeeded Hyde as Director, proposing several new ideas, including a women's studies alumnae fundraising effort, and a fellowship for a female graduate student in the arts. Pondrom also succeeded Hyde as principal investigator for the WOCC project, whose Ford funding had been renewed. However, her hope of bringing in additional research dollars through the solicitation of private funding became controversial. She left the position of Director in 1993.[59]

Working as Interim Director for one year, Susan Cook (music/women's studies) oversaw the Center's self-study (the Quality Investment Report), which asked the University to provide additional support for the WSRC. From 1994 to 1996, Dale Bauer (English/women's studies) brought an increasing emphasis on international women's studies efforts and secured a $75,000 Ford Foundation grant to internationalize the women's studies curriculum and bring gender issues into International Studies. From 1996 to 1999, Stanlie James (Afro-American Studies/women's studies) solidified many of the earlier funding programs, working to continue the emphasis on multicultural research projects, and serving as principal investigator on the Ford grant Bauer had secured. James also worked with the Frank Fellowship program for a female graduate student in the arts, a privately-endowed fellowship first created during Pondrom's tenure as Director.

* * * * *

The idea of bringing women's studies to women beyond the immediate campus had always been a central part of the women's studies mission, both in Wisconsin and nationally. The Wisconsin Idea had made the UW System a particularly hospitable place for outreach activities, as the experience of Extension faculty like Kay Clarenbach has demonstrated, but individual women's studies programs also found creative ways to express their commitment to being as inclusive as possible. Clarenbach, Connie Threinen, and Marian Thompson had been extremely active and visible on women's issues through their work with Extension, but there had not been a formal connection between their efforts and the UW-Madison Women's Studies Program. Jane Schulenburg, a Women's Studies Program member, had also developed much women's history outreach programming through her position in Outreach, but it wasn't until 1990 that the program and what was then UW-Madison Outreach created the first jointly appointed Women's Studies Outreach position.

Active in the program for more than six years as a lecturer and program member, Nancy Worcester became (and remains) the first to occupy the new role through a joint appointment between UW-Outreach and the UW-Madison Women's Studies Program. Although Clarenbach, Threinen, and Thompson had retired by this time, all three were very supportive in helping Worcester set up Women's Studies Outreach, and Jane Schulenburg played a key role in helping her develop the new programming, which included planning conferences, seminars, and workshops for a wide range of audiences in communities throughout the state.[60]

Because UW-Extension was restructured just as Worcester was hired,[61] however, she was faced with financial problems from the outset. Outreach programs now had to be more than self-supporting, bringing in sufficient revenues through the class and program fees and other sources, such as grants, to support themselves and to pay staff salaries, and this increased the pressure on Worcester to devise activities that would raise adequate revenue.[62] Despite this obstacle, Worcester—who became a tenured faculty member in 1997—organized collaborative programs such as the Domestic Violence Training Project, which offered seminars to public school and health care workers across the state, and by 1997 she had trained more than 18,000 people. Other successful efforts involved community-based health courses for women—especially women of color—which were offered at community centers, along with sexual harassment workshops, classes on menopause, and several major conferences, including ones on Women and Psychology and Women's History, sponsored jointly with other agencies.[63]

* * * * *

In many ways, the evolution of women's studies at UW-Madison mirrors the development of the field itself, from a loose group of courses taught by activist faculty, staff, and graduate students scattered across the campus to a full-fledged academic unit with a reputation for pedagogical innovation and research excellence, and a commitment to continuing its original ties to the larger community. From its beginnings, the UW-Madison Women's Studies Program has had many advantages, including a critical mass of committed participants, a relatively large budget, and support at some of the highest administrative levels. But, as we will see in Chapter 7, women at even the smallest campuses in the University of Wisconsin System devoted the same time, energy, and enthusiasm to building their own programs and departments, and continuing to develop what would become, with the founding of the Women's Studies Consortium in 1989, a unique statewide women's studies network.

Notes

1. Ellen Langill interview with Jane Piliavin.
2. Annis Pratt, "Imploding Marginality: Women's Studies and Me," unpublished essay, p. 13.
3. Ellen Langill interview with Jacqueline Macaulay.
4. Ellen Langill interviews with Diane Kravetz, Susan Stanford Friedman, and Jane Piliavin.
5. Ellen Langill interview with Susan Stanford Friedman.
6. Ellen Langill interview with Susan Stanford Friedman.
7. Personal communication, Susan Stanford Friedman to Ellen Langill, September 23, 1998.
8. Ellen Langill interviews with Jane Piliavin and Susan Stanford Friedman.
9. Ellen Langill interview with Jane Piliavin.
10. Ellen Langill interview with Jane Piliavin.
11. Ellen Langill interviews with Diane Kravetz, Susan Stanford Friedman, and Betsy Draine.
12. Personal communication, Susan Stanford Friedman to Ellen Langill, September 23, 1998.
13. Ellen Langill interviews with Jane Piliavin, Diane Kravetz, Susan Stanford Friedman, and Beverly Fruth; *Final Report of the Chancellor's Committee on Women's Studies*, May 1975, University of Wisconsin Archives; personal communication, Mariamne Whatley to Laura Stempel Mumford, December 14, 1998.
14. Program Announcement, "Ten Years of Women's Studies in Wisconsin," in UW System Women's Studies Consortium files.
15. Ruth Bleier, Diane Kravetz, and Suzanne Pingree, "News from UW-Madison," in *Feminist Collections*, Winter 1986, p. 12; Ellen Langill interviews with Elaine Marks, Diane Kravetz, and Virginia Sapiro.
16. Bleier, Kravetz, and Pingree, "News," p. 13.
17. Ellen Langill interview with Virginia Sapiro; Virginia Sapiro, "Women's Studies Program, University of Wisconsin-Madison," Report for the 1986 CIC Chairs' Meeting; Virginia Sapiro, "CIC Women's Studies Questionnaire 1986, University of Wisconsin."
18. "Classified" staff refers to Wisconsin state civil-service employees; those not subject to civil-service regulations are described as "unclassified" or, within the University, "academic" staff.
19. Personal communication, Virginia Sapiro to Laura Stempel Mumford; Ellen Langill interviews with Virginia Sapiro, Betsy Draine, Frances M. Kavenik, Jane Ewens (formerly Holbrook), Margo Anderson, and Estella Lauter.

20. Sapiro, 1986 CIC report.

21. Elizabeth White, "UW Women's Studies Improving, Lerner Says," in *Daily Cardinal*, October 5, 1988, p. 3; Ellen Langill interview with Virginia Sapiro.

22. "Professor Ruth Bleier dies of cancer at age 64," *Capital Times*, January 4, 1988.

23. Sue Rosser, "Ruth Bleier: Feminist Scientist," in Marian Swoboda, Audrey Roberts, and Jennifer Hirsch (eds.), *Women on Campus in the Eighties: Old Struggles, New Victories,* University Women: A Series of Essays (Madison: University of Wisconsin System Office of Women, 1993), Vol. IV, p. 101.

24. Ellen Langill interviews with Betsy Draine and Elaine Marks.

25. Ellen Langill interviews with Betsy Draine and Elaine Marks.

26. Ellen Langill interview with Virginia Sapiro.

27. Ellen Langill interviews with Elaine Marks and Virginia Sapiro.

28 Personal communication, Virginia Sapiro to Laura Stempel Mumford.

29. Kathryn L. Corbett and Kathleen Preston, *From the Catbird Seat: A History of Women's Studies at Humboldt State University, 1971–1996* (Arcata, CA: Humboldt State University Press, 1998), p. 54.

30. Ellen Langill interview with Susan Stanford Friedman.

31. "Motion 1 and Motion 2" for Governance Restructuring, April, 1991, Women's Studies files, UW-Madison; Ellen Langill interviews with Mariamne Whatley, Elaine Marks, and Patricia Kelleher.

32. "Governance Structure of the Women's Studies Program," April 20, 1991, University of Wisconsin, Madison; personal communication, Mariamne Whatley to Laura Stempel Mumford, September 22, 1998.

33. Ellen Langill interviews with Elaine Marks, Diane Kravetz, Mariamne Whatley, and Betsy Draine.

34. Leisa D. Meyer, Letter to Betsy Draine, May 22, 1991, in Madison files, Consortium collection.

35. Personal communication, Mariamne Whatley to Laura Stempel Mumford.

36. Jacquelyn Mitchard, "Filling in the Blanks," in *On Wisconsin*, November/December 1992, p. 25; personal communication, Mariamne Whatley to Laura Stempel Mumford.

37. Ellen Langill interview with Betsy Draine.

38. "Women's Studies Program," UW-Madison, Fall 1991, in Women's Studies Consortium files; Ellen Langill interview with Mariamne Whatley.

39. Ellen Langill interview with Donna Shalala.

40. Ellen Langill interview with Donna Shalala; personal communication, Mariamne Whatley to Laura Stempel Mumford.

41. Ellen Langill interview with Mariamne Whatley; personal communication, Mariamne Whatley to Laura Stempel Mumford.

42. Patricia King, as quoted in Catharine R. Stimpson with Nina Kressner Cobb, *Women's Studies in the United States, A Report to the Ford Foundation* (New York: Ford Foundation, 1986), p. 22.

43. "Centers for Research on Women," in *Women's Studies Newsletter* (NWSA), Vol. VII, #1, Winter 1979, p. 29.

44. "Centers for Research on Women," in *Women's Studies Newsletter*, Vol. VIII, No. 1, Winter, 1980, p. 16; Mariam K. Chamberlain, *Women in Academe: Progress and Prospects* (New York: Russell Sage Foundation, 1988), pp. 308–310.

45. Ellen Langill interview with Margo Anderson.

46. Ellen Langill interview with Margo Anderson.

47. Ellen Langill interviews with Margo Anderson, Stanlie James, and Marjorie Klein.

48. Ellen Langill interview with Elaine Marks.

49. Stimpson, p. 26; Ellen Langill interview with Marjorie Klein.

50. Ellen Langill interviews with Elaine Marks and Marjorie Klein; "Research Center to House NIMH Grant," in *Newsletter: Women's Studies Research Center*, Vol. 3, No. 2, April 1982.

51. Ellen Langill interview with Elaine Marks.

52. Ellen Langill interview with Elaine Marks.

53. "Women's Studies Research Center," brochure, 1982; Ellen Langill interview with Stanlie James.

54. Ellen Langill interviews with Stanlie James and Janet S. Hyde; "Report: Women's Studies Research Center, 1998."

55. Among the Working Papers were "Ten Years of Research on Women and Politics," by Virginia Sapiro; "New French Feminisms Ten Years Later," by Elaine Marks; "A Decade of Feminist Criticisms in the Natural Sciences," by Ruth Bleier; and "Ten Years of Historical Research on Women and Health," by Judith Leavitt (Publications of the Madison Women's Studies Research Center, 1987). A 1990 series, "A Decade of Research in Women's Studies," included essays on "Black Women in the Academy," among them "Black Professor, White University" by Nellie McKay, one of the UW-Madison's few long-standing African American members and a nationally known scholar of literature with a joint appointment in English and Afro-American Studies.

56. Ellen Langill interviews with Mariamne Whatley and Nellie McKay.

57. Stanlie James, "Report: Women Studies Research Center 1998," in Consortium files, Madison; Ellen Langill interviews with Stanlie James, Mariamne Whatley, and Janet S. Hyde; "Full Circle: The Women of Color in the Curriculum Project," WSRC Working Paper Series #16.

58. "Scholars Seek Wider Reach for Women's Studies," *New York Times*, May 17, 1989, p. 17.

59. Ellen Langill interviews with Cyrena Pondrom and Elaine Marks.

60. Personal communication, Nancy Worcester to Laura Stempel Mumford, February 24, 1999.

61. Ellen Langill interview with Nancy Worcester.

62. "Women Studies Outreach, Teaching and Organizing," pamphlet, in Women's Studies files, UW-Madison.

63. Ellen Langill interview with Nancy Worcester; "Wisconsin Domestic Violence Training Project," pamphlet, University of Wisconsin-Madison; personal communication, Mariamne Whatley to Laura Stempel Mumford.

Chapter 7

Women's Studies Around the State, 1974–1989

Although UW-Madison's Women's Studies Program is the largest in the state system, it is by no means the only one to face the kinds of struggles described in Chapter 6. But the different histories of each program and the varied characters and climates of their campuses meant that each one experienced these changes in different ways. By the mid-1980s, for example, the other early programs—at UW-Milwaukee, Whitewater, Green Bay, and Oshkosh—had also witnessed a decade of curricular development, faculty turnover, and continued budget battles, but their individual situations led to different solutions.

The **UW-Milwaukee** program was not only the state's oldest formal women's studies program, it was also one of the largest and most secure, and collaborated with other smaller programs in developing new courses. Using a 1985 grant of $13,435 from the UW System Undergraduate Teaching Improvement Council (UTIC), faculty worked with co-recipients from UW-Parkside to develop a team-taught interdisciplinary course in women's studies to be offered at the freshman/sophomore level. Reorganized as the Center for Women's Studies in 1985, with a budget home in the Graduate School, the program also managed to obtain grants from a variety of foundations for programs honoring Milwaukee women, commemorating the Milwaukee Normal School (one of the state's old teacher-education institutions), and assisting with additional course development.[1] In the mid-1980s, the Center also began to emphasize the expansion of research activities among students and faculty.[2] Yet, as a 1986 report noted, "Women's Studies at UW-M [still had] no curricular area number[3] [and depended] greatly on the number of available faculty in departments . . . to offer such courses and on the diligence and persuasiveness of the Center's staff."[4] It was not until 1994 that women's studies got its own curriculum prefix number as well as a separate number for its independent study program.[5]

Still, the Center continued to offer programming that dealt with the realities of working women's lives, including workshops such as one on "Breaking the Glass Ceiling in Higher Education" in November, 1992, which was funded by the Women's Bureau of the Department of Labor and attended by more than 90 members of the campus faculty and staff. As a follow-up to that program, Center Director Merry Weisner-Hanks was appointed in 1993 to lead a new campus task force on gender equity, an issue that became explosive after the Business School's denial of tenure to assistant professor Ceil Pillsbury, a case which received wide newspaper coverage during her subsequent lawsuit. (Pillsbury ultimately settled out of court, but succeeded in getting tenure.)[6]

While the program enjoyed a stable core of faculty, there was still a continuing problem of a too-frequent turnover in instructors. In 1990, one Center report noted that of those offering women's studies courses only three years earlier, fully 23% were no longer at the school. This turnover placed a burden upon the Director and staff of constantly recruiting new teachers to serve the more than 2,000 students who enrolled in women's studies courses each year. There was always a long list of students who could not enroll in the introductory course, and the Center sought increased funding to try to offer it more frequently, or in several sections, to accommodate the growing demand.

In the early 1990s, the Center began to present scholarship money to women's studies students through the American Association of University Women (AAUW) and awards to local middle and high school students for essays on topics concerning women, and also developed the Friends of Women's Studies, a non-profit fundraising group through which supporters could make contributions for Center activities. (At the end of the 1990s, the tradition continued with funding of Equal Education Opportunity Scholarships for low-income women whose educational opportunities had been impacted by Wisconsin's welfare reform.[7]) One of the highlights for the Center was an event in honor of its twentieth anniversary, entitled "Laverne and Shirley Hit the Books," a reference to the Milwaukee-based television characters. Held in March, 1994, and funded by the Wisconsin Humanities Council, the program featured panels, speakers, and souvenirs—commemorative mugs celebrating the success of women's studies—and many of the women who had been part of its founding were still on hand to celebrate the first two decades.[8]

In collaboration with on- and off-campus groups, the Center for Women's Studies developed a year-long outreach seminar series in 1993–94 on issues of concern to women in the trades, such as pay equity and sex discrimination. As part of a statewide outreach effort, the Women and Poverty Public Education Initiative, the Center also joined in collaborative activities with community organizations, using a $25,000 grant from the Bader Foundation to organize a public education campaign on specific issues regarding the feminization of poverty. (See Chapter 8 for more information about this initiative.)

In keeping with its position as part of an urban university, the Center maintained a close working relationship with many community women's groups and began compiling a listing of these groups in a handbook for women's activism (of which ten were produced by 1998).[9] In cooperation with the Milwaukee Jewish Federation, the Center sponsored a program on "Women Thinking Globally, Acting Locally," which served as a follow-up to the International Women's Conference in Beijing in 1995, and published a list of area women who had attended the conference in China and were available to area women's groups as speakers or resources.[10]

In 1996, with more than 30 graduate and over 100 undergraduate courses in over 25 departments across the UW-Milwaukee, the Center received approval for a

12-credit graduate certificate. More than 90 faculty and staff were affiliated with the Center by 1997, fifteen of whom had been recognized with University-wide teaching excellence awards.[11] Still, members felt that the Center's work was often invisible to campus administrators because it was not a department.[12] Even though women's studies enrolled more students than several departments in the College of Letters and Science (L&S), "Visibility of the program on the administrative radar screen continues to be an issue," reported Center Director Susan Burgess. With $10,000 in instructional support from the graduate school and a total of $10,000 from L&S, Burgess wrote, sardonically, "It seems safe to say that Women's Studies must be among the most fiscally efficient revenue producing programs on the entire campus."[13]

Although it had been one of the earliest in the country, the UW-Milwaukee Center "lag[s] behind our peers in terms of resources allocated to program development, despite the fact that our program has remained active, productive and revenue generating,"[14] causing Burgess and others to worry that it might be in jeopardy of falling behind other, better-funded programs across the country. Still, as a result of campus initiatives and as a consequence of Burgess' report, the Center ended the 1990s poised to become a department and to establish a new Women's Studies Research Center, a permanent major, and possibly a master's degree as well.[15]

* * * * *

Another of the earliest sites for women's studies in Wisconsin, the program at **UW-Whitewater**, also experienced steady growth after its founding in the mid-1970s. Administrators, students, faculty, staff, and women from the community had formed a Women's Studies Committee early in 1975 and proposed the establishment of a women's studies minor, which won approval the following year.[16] In an attempt to bring cohesion to the growing number of courses scattered through several disciplines, faculty members Sharon Tiffany, Star Olderman, and Agate Nesaule (formerly Krouse), the program's first coordinator, wrote a UTIC grant in the hopes of getting some time to plan the curriculum for the minor and to team-teach two interdisciplinary courses under the women's studies number. "Introduction to Women's Studies" and "Women, Marriage and the Family" (now "Women, Marriage and Alternatives") were team-taught during the 1977–78 academic year.

Although the grant did give the three faculty members releases from one course a semester in order to team-teach the two women's studies courses, there wasn't enough funding to buy time for planning the course or shaping the minor. The work went ahead anyway, but the year was a very intense one. Olderman vividly remembers Nesaule coming to the women's studies planning committee at the end of this very busy year with the draft of the grant's final report, which she had pulled together by writing all night, teaching her classes that day, and finally arriving at the late afternoon meeting, surprisingly energized by her incredible effort. Despite the shortage of time, at the end of the academic year, the courses had been planned and taught, new plans for further team-teaching were in place, the minor was organized, and all three faculty members survived to teach again.[17]

The next stage in program development concerned its structure: whether to remain an academic program, which would deprive members of a voice in the UW-Whitewater Faculty Council (which consisted only of department chairs) or to become a full-fledged department. In 1982, chair Ruth Schauer and the Women's Studies Committee decided to reconstitute the program as a department—one of the few women's studies programs in the UW System to make that choice.[18] The Committee also set up a procedure to screen all cross-listed courses so that department members could be assured that the women's studies content was legitimate. Unlike traditional departmental screening, the faculty were investigating not only their own departmental colleagues, but the qualifications of faculty teaching courses in other departments as well. It was a delicate political challenge, but several bad experiences convinced them that they had to be sure that no one who was covertly hostile to women's studies could offer a course, and then use the forum to undermine the new discipline.[19]

Outreach into the larger community had been an integral part of UW-Whitewater's women's studies activities since the outset, and the faculty organized a Women's Issues Committee in 1984, whose faculty, staff, students, and community members worked to establish a Women's Center, carried out annual Women's History Week activities, held programs on issues such as women's safety and women's health, sexual assault awareness, gender issues in education, and published a newsletter.[20] An ad hoc advisory committee studied ways to keep Extension's outreach programs viable, even with the budget cuts of the late 1980s. The department also established an Honorary Fellowship program in 1989, similar to that at UW-Madison, which allowed independent feminist scholars to come to campus, receiving office space and library privileges for a six-month period.[21]

In 1989, the department polled students and graduates, asking about the impact of women's studies courses on their career choices, decisions about further education, and job performance. Only about 50% of graduates felt that their women's studies minors were the main reason they got a job, but they did believe that their women's studies experience had helped them to perform better at their jobs, given them a better understanding of how people were socialized by gender, taught them to think critically, and increased their self-confidence.[22]

A 15-credit undergraduate certificate was first offered in 1984, and by 1990, the department was able to grant both B.A. and B.S. degrees in women's studies.[23] By 1993, the UW-Whitewater Women's Studies Department had twelve majors and 43 minors enrolled in its more than fifteen courses, taught by adjunct and permanent faculty. A set rotation of courses allowed both majors and minors to plan a four-year sequence of elective classes, as well as the required introductory, theory, and advanced seminar courses.[24]

* * * * *

At **UW–Green Bay**, another of the state's oldest programs benefited from a stable core faculty,[25] and the interdisciplinary nature of the UWGB concentrations of Communication and the Arts, Humanistic Studies, Social Change and Development, and Urban Studies made it especially hospitable to the overall project of integrating feminist scholarship and insights into the curriculum, helped by a 1982 initiative aimed at accomplishing that goal.[26] Still, a promising curricular climate and early progress didn't guarantee a smooth path: while a women's studies minor was first proposed in 1977 and approved soon afterwards, it began as an "extra" minor and did not actually count for graduation until 1991.[27]

Even more important, while many original members continued to play a central role, the program also faced difficulty in keeping newer women faculty on campus. The large and ongoing turnover made it difficult to establish a dependable set of courses, and funding problems threatened other successful programs, such as "Making Women Artists Known through Oral History" and the publication of *Women's Studies Research in Wisconsin*. By the late 1980s, the problem of continued faculty attrition and budget limitations caused enough concern for women's studies faculty to write to UW System Vice President Eugene Trani regarding the problem. "Like every campus, we need additional library resources," wrote Sidney Bremer and Estella Lauter, "and [have] insufficient faculty resources to mount innovative programs [or] outreach efforts."[28]

In late 1988, the Women's Studies Program at UW-Green Bay received approval from the Faculty Senate as a "codified academic unit," a designation that gave the program more flexibility in creating and cross-listing courses, and contributed to becoming a more stable self-governing unit. Increased budgetary support came from the new Dean of Liberal Arts and Sciences, Carol Pollis, who saw women's studies as a vital part of the academic program. She believed that the faculty at UW-Green Bay were attracted to the campus because of its multidisciplinary. "A lot of people who have been here for a long time, working in an interdisciplinary environment, take it for granted."[29] By the fall of 1992, the hiring of several new women faculty also boosted the program's participants to twelve for the first time, and in that same year, the first separate expenses budget was provided, although there was still no release time for the program chair and no permanent office or program center.

Ever since the 1981 closing of the Lucy Stone Women's Center, there had been no physical focus to the program and scant room to house its growing resource collection. One commentator noted poignantly, "women's studies has operated as a campus bellwether for women's problems . . . yet has developed an extraordinary record on campus, sponsoring community forums, campus conferences, and task forces on women's issues."[30]

The growth in course enrollments was steady, with the number increasing from around 200 in 1988 to over 540 students by the fall of 1992, yet, as the program's 1993 self-study noted, "We have no facilities, not even . . . a key of our own to the Women's Center that holds the filing cabinet containing our program minutes and documents. We have depended on the good will of our participating concentrations for supplies, expenses, and secretarial services to support the courses and our program management."[31] There was, however, one bright spot: "the library staff has been very responsive to faculty requests for books about women and gender issues . . . and presented us with a list of over 200 relevant books ordered in the previous two years."[32]

* * * * *

UW-Oshkosh's experience also makes it clear that simply reaching such apparently significant stages as the establishment of a women's studies minor doesn't guarantee coherence. When it was approved, the UW-Oshkosh minor—the first in the state—was to be administered by a Faculty Council system, but without the central planning provided by a formal program, and with faculty not always able to offer specific courses, it was difficult at first to maintain the focus of a nine-course minor and to gather a solid core of either faculty or students. The following fall, Leta DiSalvo became the program's first coordinator, holding the minor together for one year without any release time or compensation.[33]

Things improved in the fall of 1976, however, when the University rehired Barbara Sniffen, who had previously taught history on campus but had been laid off. Sniffen served as the program's coordinator for the next ten years, with a quarter-time salary and no support staff. (She also continued to teach a course on "The Images of Women in Western Civilization" through Interdisciplinary Studies.) A small group of women faculty—who, like the original program founders, called themselves the Women's Studies Committee—was formed to assist the coordinator and to help in overseeing the course offerings.[34]

* * * * *

While these early-established programs and departments faced the challenges of growth and expansion, for other programs across the UW System, the late 1970s and 1980s were a period of initial program development. Once again, the individual character of each UW System institution shaped the local development of women's studies.

At the **UW-Platteville**, women faced an obstacle that the System's other institutions did not: Because of its longstanding identity as a bastion of the traditional male specialties of mining and engineering, the students and faculty were predominantly men. Established through the merging of one of the state's Normal Schools for teacher education and its first mining school (the Wisconsin Mining Trade School, which eventually became the Wisconsin Institute of Technology), the Platteville campus climate continued to reflect its mining history. As one description of the school noted, "Even when a girl was occasionally enrolled at the mining school, the main force of activity and progression still remained masculine."[35]

Despite being vastly outnumbered, though, the women faculty were able to begin organizing in the early 1970s, helped, as so many women around Wisconsin were, by visits from UW-Madison activists Ruth Bleier and Joan Roberts. UW-Platteville's situation was not unique in the U.S.; nevertheless, it presented special problems to those trying to establish women's studies and feminist education at UW-Platteville.

In a sense, women's studies began there in the summer of 1971, four months before the official establishment of the WCCWHE, when the Department of Political Science sponsored a two-week workshop entitled "Freedom and Equality for Women: Toward Liberation." Included in the sessions, which were open to teachers from kindergarten through college, were lectures, panel discussions, and workshops on a variety of women's issues, with speakers ranging from Kay Clarenbach (UW-Extension and NOW) to Catherine Conroy from the Communication Workers of America.

The July event was an overwhelming success, but just as on the other campuses around the state, the formal organization of a women's studies program took several more years, and it was not until the fall of 1975 that a group of women faculty who called themselves the Status of Women Committee called for the development of a women's studies program on campus. Throughout the 1975–76 academic year, the group, led by Barbara Parsons (philosophy), Jacqueline Ross (English), Robert Olsen (English), and Helen Tierney (history), worked to steer the proposal through the required campus committees and to obtain the approval of the Vice Chancellor.[36] By the fall of 1976, just two years after the report of the UW System Task Force on Women's Studies, the program was formally established, with Ross as the interim chair. The Women's Studies Council—as the Committee was now called—believed that the peculiar position of women on the UW-Platteville campus seemed to require someone schooled in local campus politics, and Ross soon became the program's first permanent chair, with a quarter-time release.[37]

Once the program was established, it served to unify the campus's diverse women's studies offerings with formal course-approval, fixed requirements, and a regular schedule. The earliest courses, such as "Contemporary Issues: Psychology of Human Sexuality," "Thematic Studies in Literature," and "Issues in History: Women in History," had been offered on a rotating basis since the Fall of 1971, but were now organized into an interdisciplinary program that included an "Introduction to Women's Studies" pre-requisite that involved students in the basic scholarly questions posed in the new interdisciplinary field of women's studies. Growing alongside the program was a campus women's center, also founded in 1976, with its director serving on the program's governing Council. As a result, the two were more closely linked than on many other campuses, and were able to work together to sponsor and publicize events for women.

Yet even as these successes were being celebrated, efforts to defuse some of the blatant sexism on campus were less successful. During preparations for both the 1975 and 1976 homecoming parades, for instance, several floats displayed explicitly anti-feminist slogans, including one which had the banner, "Keep your women barefoot, pregnant, and out of the mine," a reference to the campus's history as a mining school. Protests by women were met with defensive letters to the editor in the campus paper, but nothing was done to prevent the floats from being part of the homecoming parades. In 1976, two women—Barbara Parsons and one of her students, Donna Gibbs—stood along the parade route and responded to the worst of the floats by throwing raw eggs at them as they passed by. As one member of the egg brigade later admitted, her "early training as a ballplayer" was extremely useful in giving her deadly aim with the eggs: Neither she nor the friend with her "threw like a girl!"[38]

Another incident suggested that women needed to struggle not only against a hostile campus climate, but against their own deeply engrained sense of appropriate behavior. Historian Helen Tierney, one of the founders of UW-Platteville's Women's Studies Program, was nominated by her colleagues to serve as chair of the history department, customarily decided by a majority vote. During the balloting, she modestly declined to vote for herself, and when the tally was announced, it was discovered that she had received all but one vote—her own. However, a program member recalled after Tierney died in 1998, the Chancellor "called Helen in to tell her that there was no way he could approve a woman as department chair unless he had a unanimous vote."[39] Several years later, Tierney did become department chair, and later also served as chair of women's studies when Jackie Ross's long tenure in the position ended.

* * * * *

UW-Parkside in Kenosha was one of two new four-year universities (the other was UW-Green Bay) established by legislative act in 1965, and although there were more female than male students on the Parkside campus, there were very few women on the faculty. The first person to offer a women's studies course there was Carole Vopat, who had completed her Ph.D. degree in English studying, like most scholars of the period, the traditional white male writers. Vopat recalled reading *Sexual Politics* by Kate Millett and realizing with a "click!" that her education had failed to open doors for her into the world of women writers and women's perspectives on literature.[40]

In the fall of 1971, she began to offer "Women's Liberation and Literature," and in 1972 she added seminars on "Images of Women in Literature" and "Modern Women Writers." By the end of 1972, a small group of women had established the UW-Parkside Women's Caucus, which was connected to the Kenosha branch of the National Organization for Women (NOW), and in April 1973, the two groups sponsored a Women's Day celebration at which Vopat delivered the keynote address, "Anatomy is Not Destiny."[41]

The UW-Parkside feminists were loudly criticized by several male colleagues and some outspoken male students, who accused Vopat in particular of a variety of outrages, including "arrogance" and lesbianism—the latter a standard weapon in attempts to denigrate feminists. Yet despite this harassment, and in part because of the growing voice of the WCCWHE around the UW System, the Parkside campus began to hire more women—although many, like historian Angela Howard Zophy, were in ad hoc rather than permanent positions. Unofficially, and therefore with no release time and no budget, Vopat (who had been granted early tenure in 1974) coordinated the few women's studies courses, and as more women joined the faculty, she also became unofficially responsible for writing an affirmative action plan and mentoring women faculty. Together, several other feminists—including Vopat's English department colleague Carol Lee Saffioti (now Saffioti-Hughes) and historian Bonnie Smith—formed the Women's Studies Committee and began to plan for a program of their own, following the recommendations of the 1974 UW System Task Force Report.[42]

In 1978, the first "Introduction to Women's Studies"—a two-semester course cross-listed in English and history—was offered at UW-Parkside, team-taught by Vopat and Smith, and there were sufficient additional courses for Saffioti to write a proposal for a minor in women's studies. The proposal received approval in the spring of 1979, and the formal program began with Vopat as coordinator. Women's studies became one of the first programs on campus to offer courses focusing on American minorities and, later, gay and lesbian literature.[43]

As on many campuses, a new pattern of female leadership also emerged among the students, who often went on to work in fields related to their work in women's studies. One former UW-Parkside women's studies student, Theresa Reinders, later became the coordinator of the campus Women's Center, which began to lobby on non-academic issues such as abortion rights. The issue of childcare also became a growing concern for both faculty and students, as the Parkside campus struggled with funding on-site facilities and for extended hours to accommodate students with later classes or faculty with meetings that lasted past 4:30 p.m. The campus's distance from the two local communities of Racine and Kenosha made on-site daycare an even greater necessity for many.

The early ties between campus women and the local women's movement proved to be a strength of the Parkside program, as at UW-Whitewater and UW-Green Bay. Women from the Kenosha and Racine communities were represented on the Women's Studies Steering Committee. Together, these community women and the campus group sponsored a yearly conference on women's issues, beginning in 1979. (For instance, in 1985, the "Women and Work Conference" was held at the nearby Wingspread Center and co-sponsored by the Racine-based Johnson Foundation.)

Having created the first interdisciplinary minor at UW-Parkside, members of the women's studies program had to defend the intellectual substance of the program, along with the integrity of their own scholarly research. As was true on campuses across Wisconsin and throughout the country, many faculty who resisted the program's development viewed women's studies as a passing trend rather than a serious academic program. Ironically, however, the program became a model for the development of other interdisciplinary programs at UW-Parkside, such as International Studies, Ethnic Studies, and the Interdisciplinary Studies/Weekend College.[44] From being cast as a pariah, the Women's Studies Program had become a paradigm.

However, another decade passed before the program received financial support through the institution of a third-time release for the coordinator in 1988. Until then, as with many other programs on campuses across the state, the women's studies coordinator worked as a volunteer, taking on all of the duties as an overload, and relying upon the tacit support of her department for necessary clerical assistance. With no permanent office, the program floated from place to place, wherever the coordinator was housed in her own department,[45] and it was another ten years before the program received the money to hire a part-time project assistant in 1998.

In the UW-Parkside Women's Studies Program, two of the members of our steering committee, Carole Vopat (English) and Evelyn Zepp (French), are instrumental in mentoring Women's Studies faculty, regardless of field, through the tenure process. They are particularly helpful in giving suggestions about how to present one's research to those outside as well as inside the field, to make it clearer for those unfamiliar with women-centered research.

Feminist pedagogy, a teaching style which gives students more responsibility for the class, is far different from the traditional lecture style which used to be the norm. Lisa Kornetsky visited classes of new Women's Studies faculty and wrote helpful analyses of their teaching methods which assisted their departments in understanding why such pedagogical approaches made sense. As director of the campus Teaching Center, she was able to provide legitimacy to these innovative teaching styles.

Women's Studies faculty must get tenure in disciplinary departments outside Women's Studies. They are often by far the youngest members of their departments, often the only women, and sometimes the only people of color. The Women's Studies Program at UW-Parkside gives the Women's Studies faculty access to faculty across the campus, and a diverse set of colleagues with whom to share ideas.

I remember when none of the major faculty committees at UW-Parkside had any women members. The Women's Studies faculty strategized to encourage women to stop volunteering for minor committees such as parking and volunteer only to run for major committees until we felt that women were being represented in important decision making on the faculty. At an extremely contentious meeting of the entire faculty, Lana Rakow (Communication and Women's Studies) proposed a rule stating that the gender composition of each faculty committee should be reported annually, to make the inequities more visible. This passed by a small margin. This was in 1991. In 1998, the University Committee is chaired by Frances Kavenik, a former director of Women's Studies, and women are well represented on all major committees. However, there is a definite revolving door pattern among women faculty and administrators, especially women of color, which we are now trying to address by focusing on the climate for women within departments.

—Mary Kay Schleiter

* * * * *

The first two women's studies courses at the **UW-La Crosse**, offered in the spring semester of 1973, were "History of Women in the United States" and "Women in Society," an anthropology course, and in the following year, the first literature course, "Major Authors: American Women Writers," was approved. The core of leadership on campus centered on the faculty teaching these first three courses: Susannah Lloyd (anthropology), Vivian Munson (history), and Joan Yeatman (English). (Yeatman also became active very early in WCCWHE, and was its coordinator in 1972, as well as serving on the System Task Force on Women's Studies.[46])

Despite these early courses, though, the faculty only began to work in earnest on women's studies course development in the spring of 1975. Just after the 1974 Task Force report was issued, Jean Foss, the UW-La Crosse Affirmative Action Officer (who later became Vice Chancellor), convened a campus women's studies task force to plan a program. Beginning with the assertion that "Women's Studies is basic to the educational mission of the university, both as a corrective and as a field of study in its own right," the new group moved forward very quickly, helped by the impetus of the System report and by news of developments on other campuses,[47] and the Institute for Women's Studies was approved in the fall of 1975.

Plans were made to inaugurate the new Institute in January 1976, with a required "Introduction to Women's Studies" course, and with Judith Green as the first coordinator, the Institute also managed to get funding for a campus Women's Resource Center.[48] The predictable backlash came at the end of this first year, 1975–76, when the center became the target of criticism, attacked with the often-posed question: "Why do you need a Women's Resource Center? There isn't a Men's Resource Center." The women, however, were ready with what had become the standard response, underlining the biases of the traditional male-dominated curriculum: "Oh, yes, there is," they replied, indicating the main UW-La Crosse library: "It's called Murphy Library."[49]

During the late 1970s, a growing commitment to women's studies brought as many as twenty faculty to the program for at least one course, and heightened interest in team-teaching the multidisciplinary introductory course. Two years after its establishment, the position of coordinator was upgraded to half-time (Vivian Munson, 1977–79), and with this stronger administrative support, the program began to publish its first newsletter in 1977 and worked toward getting approval for a 15-credit women's studies certificate (1979). In 1980, the Institute's administrator position was increased to three-quarter time (Carol Levine, 1979–82), making it one of the programs with the greatest funded commitment. A national search for the new Director of Women's Studies resulted in the 1982 hiring of Cara Chell.[50]

Aware of the need to reach out into the community and to involve their own students more fully in the program, Institute members established a Women's Studies Student Association, and a new half-time position for program development was created in 1983. The Association planned brown bag lunches that focused on the concerns and needs of women students, and the program planned public functions that would reach out to community women, including speakers, discussions, an "Evening of Women's Creative Writing," and a competition for student essays.[51]

The creation of a 24-credit minor ran into major barriers when the UW-La Crosse Faculty Senate at first refused approval (finally granted in December 1986) for what it called a "one person, one academic position" program, and urged the Institute to consider reconstituting itself into a department, which would allow it to make direct faculty hires and receive a more substantial budget line. Departmental status, which came in January 1987, allowed the women's studies faculty to have a greater voice in University governance through direct representation on University committees and in the Faculty Senate. However, there were also disadvantages, because, while becoming a department brought with it two full-time faculty positions and broader governance powers, it also meant the loss of the funding for community outreach it had enjoyed as a program.[52]

Nevertheless, the department maintained its longstanding commitment to outreach programming, creating the Single Parent Self-Sufficiency Program (SPSSP), a program established in 1988 to help low-income single parents (primarily women) gain access to higher education through a variety of support services and academic preparation in critical thinking skills. Other examples of that commitment to outreach include the department's collaboration with the SPSSP and the city of La Crosse to develop a mentoring program for people—again, primarily women—affected by Wisconsin's 1997 welfare-reform initiative. Also, notes chair Sandra Krajewski, "*equally* we value our attempts and eventually our success in offering interdisciplinary courses as well as a multidisciplinary curriculum."[53]

* * * * *

The first women's studies courses offered at **UW-Eau Claire** came from women faculty members in the departments of religion, sociology, and English. After meeting with Ruth Bleier and Joan Roberts in the fall of 1971, several of them enthusiastically joined forces with the new WCCWHE and soon took leadership roles in the statewide movement. Edna Hood, Nadine St. Louis, Carol Fairbanks, and Sarah Harder had all joined the Eau Claire faculty during the late 1960s and early 1970s, and formed the nucleus of a very active and visible group that worked not only to establish the campus program, but in statewide activities as well. In the spring of 1972, UW-Eau Claire hosted a WCCWHE meeting, a gathering participants remembered as intensive, goal-oriented, and highly informative, but also as very joyous, and Eau Claire faculty and staff continued to be active in statewide work, with Sarah Harder serving on the 1974 UW System Task Force on Women's Studies, and Edna Hood elected co-chair of WCCWHE.[54]

Early UW-Eau Claire courses included "The Sociology of Women," "Images of Women in Literature," and "Women in Religion," and in 1975, the Women's Studies Committee supervised the creation of a formal women's studies program, despite an atmosphere of only "passive support" from administrators.[55] The approval of new core courses was delayed repeatedly, and there were no decisions made about how to list the courses, or where to house the new program.[56] Finally, in 1977, Carol Fairbanks became the first coordinator, publicizing the new program before course registration began for the following semester. Although the English department, Fairbanks' academic home, voted to house the program, the administration rejected this plan, again leaving the program without a base.[57] The courses filled rapidly, but solid administrative support was still lacking. In an attempt to reach out to male students, Fairbanks publicized the fact that "Women's

Studies is not for Women Only!" As Hood told the student newspaper, at least the male students were now treating women's studies as less of a joke than they had in earlier years, even though course enrollments remained overwhelmingly female.[58]

Another effort, spearheaded by Fairbanks, was the creation of the Helen X. Sampson Collection in the McIntyre University Library at UW-Eau Claire, officially opened in February 1978. Named for an English professor emeritus, the collection contained a variety of publications and research materials related to women's studies, and was housed in the Women's Bibliographic Center, a separate room in the library.[59]

As early as 1978, the UW-Eau Claire program had gotten approval for a topical minor, which became a 24-credit women's studies minor in 1984. That same year, Sarah Harder became coordinator, a position she retains today, and her long tenure suggests the stamp an individual member can put on a program. Harder had taught an early "Images of Women in Literature" course for several semesters, served as the campus Affirmative Action Officer, and worked with The Association of University Professors (TAUP) to achieve passage of a provision that provided sick leave to women who gave birth.[60]

Harder recalls the inspiration Kay Clarenbach provided, both through her visits to the Eau Claire campus and through her national activism. Harder, whose involvement with the American Association of University Women (AAUW) led her into the national arena at the 1977 International Women's Year Conference in Houston, was part of the small delegation that presented the Houston "Plan of Action for Women" to President Jimmy Carter, and like many faculty and staff active in women's studies around the state, she also became prominent in statewide feminist groups (as first chair of the Wisconsin Women's Council and a founder of the Wisconsin Women's Network) and in national professional organizations (as president of AAUW in 1985). Harder also created a campus re-entry program for returning adult women at UW-Eau Claire called the "Next Step Program," much as Clarenbach had in Madison.[61]

Internationalism had long been part of the UW-Eau Claire program, and Harder brought an even greater focus to it. As early as 1979, the campus had sponsored a conference entitled "An International Round Table on American Women: Stereotypes Around the World," with Ugandan anthropologist Christine Obo as the featured panelist.[62] Harder was also prominent in establishing connections between Wisconsin women's studies practitioners and women in the former Soviet Union (see Chapter 8).

Initiated in 1983, "Challenges and Choices" career workshops have brought girls from across the region together with women professionals. Widely replicated across the state, this program inspired the state's Choices Initiative for girls from the Wisconsin Women's Council. As AAUE President, Harder also launched its research and advocacy focus on girls. AAUW's 1992 "How America's Schools Shortchange Girls" and subsequent reports resulted in nationwide attention to educational equity for girls. In the mid-'90s, an outreach program brought "Challenges and Choices" career programming into the middle schools of sixteen regional school districts.[63]

Like other women's studies faculty around the state, members of the UW-Eau Claire program also worked to reach out to community women. Early in the program's history, faculty women in the English department offered a series of one-credit courses to community women through the UW-Extension, and the Arts and Sciences Outreach faculty offered seminars entitled "Beyond Feminism" and "Non-Verbal Communication for the Working Woman." In the late 1980s, a "Women in Transition" (WIT) program was developed to help make higher education more accessible to low-income women,[64] along with a three-part video series.[65]

* * * * *

The **UW-Stevens Point** experience of Alice Randlett exemplifies the impact of women's studies on individual women's lives. In the fall of 1970, Randlett arrived at the campus as a new librarian and enrolled the next semester in a new course, "Women and Literature," taught by Nancy Moore. The material resonated with her, as it did with many other students, and this first experience in women's studies became a moment of consciousness-raising that changed her life.[66] Randlett soon joined the small group of faculty and staff women who were holding discussion groups on feminist issues, and like many others, became interested in the new WCCWHE. Soon after, faculty member Mary Jo Buggs invited members of the Stevens Point faculty and staff to plan for and attend a meeting of the statewide group, which occurred in 1972.[67] (Buggs herself became the campus representative to the WCCWHE, and its statewide co-chair in 1972–73.)

The issue of domestic violence was a flashpoint for the development of support for other feminist projects on the UWSP campus. As one woman administrator at the campus recalled, "there were no shelters for abused women, no centers or homes of any kind where they could escape the violence."[68] When such a shelter was proposed for the campus in 1974, the Vice Chancellor mandated that it be housed in the Home Economics Management House, where majors learned to sew, dust, and cook. However, the faculty manager of the Home Economics House was a traditional home economics disciple, and a confrontation occurred between those championing old and new roles for women. Although the shelter was established, for several years it competed for parking, facility usage, and respect with the home economics faculty, who saw no reason or justification for having a group of feminists or victims of abuse intrude into their once-peaceful department home.

When the 1974 System Task Force report was released, UW-Stevens Point faculty received the first official response from local administrators on the subject of women's studies: that such a program should be established because of the

Regents' recommendation, and in November 1975, the Vice Chancellor appointed four faculty members to begin planning it. The new Women's Studies Committee was also given the power to secure the program's first chair and to institute a minor, and the program officially began the following year, with Joan Taylor as its first coordinator and plans for a minor finalized.[69]

The program's purpose was threefold: to "raise women's perceived value and women's own aspirations," to "improve our understanding of women's lives," and to "empower students to take control of their own lives and to work to improve the human condition through an understanding of the impact on our lives of gender . . . race, class, sexual orientation and age."[70] The earliest existing courses—including "Women in Literature" (first taught in 1971), "Special Topics: Women's Liberation as a Social Movement" (1972), and "American Women in History" (1973)—were now incorporated into a full-scale program that grew over the next few years to include more than twenty ongoing courses. As on other System campuses, women's studies classes at UW-Stevens Point regularly filled during the first week of registration.

The position of women's studies coordinator brought with it quarter-time release, a pattern that had become typical at many of Wisconsin's four-year campuses. However, at UW-Stevens Point, this release was granted for only one semester each year,[71] and the budget did not allow for support staff, which had to be supplied by the coordinator's home department. The Women's Studies Program was also not allotted any office space, which made it difficult to heighten its campus visibility. Instead, as on many UW campuses, it was located wherever the coordinator's departmental office existed, and it therefore moved around the campus with each change in leadership.[72]

* * * * *

UW-Stout, in Menomonie, has an unusual history within the UW System. Originally founded in 1893 as a private college, it became a state institution in 1911, and in 1955, joined the Wisconsin State Colleges system—which in turn became part of the UW System in the 1971 merger. Traditionally, UW-Stout offered few liberal arts majors, and its programs emphasized technical education, home economics, and hotel management.[73]

While UW-Stout had begun to offer several courses on women as early as the fall of 1973 ("Women Writers," followed by "Images of Women in Literature" and "Introduction to Women's Studies" the following spring), few new ones were added for several years. In the campus report submitted to the 1974 System Task Force on Women's Studies, one clause suggests that some of this curriculum was not expected to become permanent, but was designed to fulfill specific student needs: The description of "The Role of Women in American Society," offered in the Department of Education, stated that it would continue to be taught only "until it is no longer requested by students."

Nevertheless, faculty experimented with feminist pedagogy in otherwise traditional courses. "Human Sexual Biology," originally created by another faculty member but later taught by Fran Garb, was controversial in part because of the teaching strategies Garb used, such as discussions, group work, and individual presentations, as well as the standard lecture approach. She also tried new ways to make the women students become more involved, since they were in the minority and were less confident of themselves as scientists. After conducting a survey about styles of learning and approaches to the subject matter, Garb rearranged her classroom in order to change its climate. She seated the male students around the edges and in the rear, partly to keep them from sitting together in the center and intimidating the women students. She then seated the few women students closer to the front, where their voices could be heard and where they would not be put off by comments or glances of disapproval from their male peers. If this represented special catering to the women students, Garb recalls, she believed it was justified by the results, a more equitable classroom climate and more participation from the women students.[74]

In the spring of 1976, Janet Polansky of the English department worked with a small committee to prepare a proposal for a program and a minor. Just as the proposal was being defended before the Faculty Senate, the news of Priscilla Timper's tenure denial shocked the campus. The retention of qualified faculty women who were important to the women's studies became part of their battle.[75]

A major debate about the establishment of women's studies on the Stout campus concerned which school should house a program. Both home economics and Liberal Studies were considered as homes, but with the strong urging of the Women's Studies Committee, it became part of UW-Stout's School of Liberal Studies, the university's largest college.[76] Approval of the program came in late 1976 and Janet Polansky became its first coordinator in the spring of 1977, although with only a quarter-time release and virtually no budget. In fact, the release-time support was later withdrawn and the position of coordinator became entirely an overload. In that first year, the annual allocation to support Polansky's travel to the semiannual coordinators' meetings in Madison and the annual System conference, and for all other office and incidental expenses—including Women's History Month activities—was $1,000. Polansky served in the position for twelve years, and when she returned to it in 1996, the budget was the same $1,000 it had been twenty years before![77]

A virtue of small women's studies programs such at UW-Stout's, with no more than three or four minors each year, was that they remained very closely connected to women's groups within the community. Smaller programs needed the energy of community groups more than some larger campus programs, which often pulled away from their community support as they matured and became more solidly institutionalized within the university. Women in the Menomonie community attended the Women's Studies Program's brown bag lunch series, came to conferences, served on committees to plan the events of Women's History Month in March each year, and provided support for the program and its public events.[78]

Because of the curricular mission of the Stout campus, which emphasized practical education, the Women's Studies Program there faced special challenges. The program had to be titled "Women's Studies: Theory and Practical Applications," although 15 of its 22 courses were offered through Arts and Sciences, including "Introduction to Women's Studies," several feminist literature courses, and a "Women in Art" course taught by Mary Hovind.[79] The remainder of the 22-credit minor required students to choose from "practical or applied" courses, such as "Assertiveness Training," "Focus on Leadership," "Logic," and "Women and the Law." These courses dovetailed with the campus's emphasis on applied education and offered practical and women-centered rather than theoretical and strongly feminist content.

The faculty also obtained a UTIC grant for a "Gender-Balancing Across the Curriculum" program,[80] and in 1984 hosted the annual Systemwide women's studies conference, whose theme that year was "Women and Technology." (One outgrowth of the conference was a popular new course called "Gender and Technology.") Other courses, such as "Women, Minorities, and Management" and "The Workplace and the Family," were directed at the campus's many business majors.[81] When the Regents recommended that each campus create its own women's studies program, few may have realized how diverse the programs that emerged would be, but the growth of Stout's Women's Studies Program demonstrates how the different curricular flavor of each campus shaped their individual development.

One aspect of the women's studies experience at UW-Stout is that it was really a bottom-up development; that is, it was instigated by students and faculty interest was drummed up later. There was an active women's consciousness raising group in Menomonie that consisted of students and I believe some community women. The group got so popular that it began to get larger than the original members preferred. (I came in on it when it was becoming overgrown and didn't get to know the original members really well.)

One of the outgrowths of the conversations was a desire for a course in women's studies. I don't think any faculty members were involved, or the group wouldn't have come to me. I was then a member of the classified staff in the UW-Stout library, but since

> *I had a master's degree in American history, I was deemed quali-*
> *fied to bring a course to the curriculum committee and act as the*
> *first instructor. We conducted the course as an interdisciplinary*
> *offering (partly to avoid the perennial contests between Sociology*
> *and Home Economics about the proper home of anything they*
> *both claimed and partly because we didn't have a department*
> *member to teach it).*
>
> *I taught one or two sessions on women in history (I blush to tell*
> *you, but I did a lot of research in the area, and I think I gave them*
> *an okay introduction) and the other sessions had guest speakers—*
> *psychology of women, health issues, women in literature, gender*
> *equity in education, etc. These were a combination of women from*
> *the community who had been involved in the consciousness raising*
> *group and women faculty at Stout who were willing to come in as a*
> *guest for one session. One was an elementary school teacher who*
> *shared her concerns about the biases in children's literature; one*
> *was a Carleton alum who lived on a communal farm in rural Dunn*
> *County—in other words, a real mix.*
>
> *—Mary Richards*

* * * * *

Alone among the System's campuses, **UW-Superior** did not list any women's studies courses when it was surveyed by the 1974 System Task Force, but two years later, a committee was established to begin a study of possible women's studies courses and to plan a program. Led by Delores Harms and Lydia Binger, this group worked to generate more student and faculty awareness of the importance of women's studies. Their report outlined an interdisciplinary minor, including courses in art, communications, English, history, psychology, political science, and teacher education.[82] The minor was officially approved on November 18, 1976, and the committee moved forward to implement the new program. They also created a separate Wisconsin Idea Committee to work on implementation of one of the program's strongest goals: to bring community women into women's studies through continuing education activities.

The program got off to a slow start, with small enrollments in the courses, often no more than ten students a semester. An Extended Degree program was created in 1978, along with a new concentration in its graduate program for counseling women, and a collaborative women's network was developed with other campuses in the Lake Superior region, including Northland College, St. Scholastica, and Mt.

Senario College.[83] Another aid to the program's visibility was the development of a Women's Resource Center, which collected articles and publications about women's studies and about other programs into one central location. Moreover, the large number of women students receiving degrees in physical education led to another campus emphasis, women's studies courses offered as part of the PE major.

Another gauge of the changing campus climate for women students at Superior was the great increase in the number of women on the faculty. For fifty years, between 1913 (when the first woman faculty member, Ellen Clark, was hired) and 1963, the campus had hired only nineteen women total. However, between 1963 and 1990, the total number of women hired onto the faculty numbered 71.

* * * * *

Created in 1965 from the former Extension Centers, the **UW Center System** (now the **University of Wisconsin Colleges**) eventually grew to include thirteen two-year campuses across the state. These campuses have a unique administrative structure: each department is spread across thirteen separate homes. Geographically separated and newly created, the Centers faced particular challenges in planning and implementing unified programs. However, faculty at the Centers also enjoyed a measure of independence not always present at the larger university campuses. Because most of the campuses are rural, they serve as the cultural centers of their communities. Faculty interested in women's studies frequently became key members of these communities; they were able to initiate women's studies programming and courses that were uniquely responsive to community needs.

From the beginning in 1973, a remarkable number of disciplines in the Centers—English, philosophy, psychology, sociology/anthropology, history, and political science—developed women's studies courses. Some of these courses met with questions from colleagues, who often trivialized the material. For example, one women's studies professor was informed by departmental colleagues that there wouldn't be enough material for her course to last one week, much less fill a textbook. Others encountered similar skepticism, but they answered their critics by creating strong academic courses that have been offered regularly for 25 years.

To address the problems of geographic dispersion and the fact that most Centers campuses had only one or two people teaching women's studies courses, the UW System Administration's Karen Merritt convened a special conference in the spring of 1976, attended by representatives from eleven of the thirteen Centers campuses. The immediate outcome was the establishment of a women's studies working group for the Centers. The committee outlined its goals as "developing Women's Studies courses which would transfer into four-year programs, monitoring special topics courses in Women's Studies, and developing a bibiliography of holdings in the area of Women's Studies available in Centers libraries."[84] The number of women's studies courses increased, gradually including more disciplines, more campuses, and more faculty.

In 1985, the Colleges Faculty Senate Curriculum Committee approved the addition of "Women's Studies 101 (Introduction)" and six additional cross-listed courses. An official Women's Studies Program Committee, chaired by Jane Ewens, was also established to screen and monitor courses. The current Colleges catalogue lists nine women's studies courses; there are also several new Interdisciplinary Studies courses which involve Women's Studies faculty team-teaching across disciplines and via distance education technology. The Colleges women's studies faculty and staff hold semi-annual conferences that allow them to share research and teaching experiences. Although sometimes awkward, the geographical dispersion of the Colleges has made both diversity and collaboration inevitable. Colleges faculty in women's studies continue their history of being creatively responsive to unique campus communities.[85]

* * * * *

According to the survey of Wisconsin campuses conducted as part of the System Task Force's work in 1974, **UW-River Falls** had initiated several women's studies courses three years earlier and had offered them continually, with enrollments at more than capacity. The "Women in Literature" and "Women in Contemporary Society" courses had first opened the doors to students on campus in 1971, and were supplemented by the less frequent offerings "Racial and Cultural Minorities" and "Advanced Intergroup Relations," both taught from a feminist perspective.[86]

Still, however popular these courses were, there was no concerted effort to bring them together into a formal women's studies program for fourteen more years. However, students did have the option of designing their own individualized programs. This option was cited as evidence that UW-River Falls conformed to the Task Force recommendation. When faculty member Laura Quinn was sent, as a substitute for the campus affirmative action officer, to the yearly meeting of the UW women's studies administrators in 1984, she learned that every four-year and doctoral campus in the System had a women's studies program of some kind—except River Falls.

"I made myself obnoxious over the next several months," wrote Quinn, "with my everybody-except-for-us-has-one grievance."[87] Earlier efforts to establish a program had met with both active and passive resistance and Quinn, too, was repeatedly told that, since UW-River Falls did have courses on women, there was no problem. Still, the issue was a full-scale women's studies program with coherence, leadership, and planning, and finally, as a result of Quinn's lobbying efforts and with the support of a few core faculty members (both men and women), the

UW-River Falls administration agreed to take action, a campus task force was convened, and both course and program development moved forward rapidly.

Because of the historic conflation of affirmative action with women's studies at UW-River Falls, one of the first steps was to officially separate the two, in what Quinn called an "amicable divorce."[88] During the 1985–86 academic year, two introductory courses, the program plan, and a women's studies minor were approved and prepared for launching, and a Women's Resource Center was established. Quinn credited many groups for the fast "catch-up" at River Falls. Meetings with women's studies coordinators from other campuses gave her a volume of information about existing programs, budgets, curriculum and leadership patterns within the UW System. "There was much to be said for being the thirteenth campus, strategically," she later wrote, using Annette Koldony's famous metaphor: "So many others had danced through the minefield and could offer dance lessons and mine maps."[89]

* * * * *

Despite the enormous advances described in this chapter, women's studies faced an ongoing struggle for equity, scholarly recognition, and legitimacy within the academy. In 1985, Elaine Marks appeared before the University of Wisconsin Board of Regents and responded to the question of where the field of women's studies was headed after its first ten years of formal existence, and her remarks still apply more than ten years later.

Marks began optimistically, noting that "women's studies as a field and feminism as a discourse that informs the field now occupy a visible place both within the institutions of higher learning and within the intellectual arena of competing discourse in the United States." With more than 450 women's studies programs and over 40 research centers in the U.S. alone, Marks emphasized the importance of institutional independence that would allow women's studies to "grapple with many new intellectual challenges and continuing inquiries in the years ahead. Autonomous women's studies programs are absolutely essential to the vitality of this enterprise."[90] Still, Marks told the Regents that women's studies remained an "embattled field," and that much of its work was still to be accomplished. It was not yet clear how traditional disciplines would be transformed by feminist inquiries, or how new methodologies might assist in understanding how women's experiences have differed from men's. "Because feminism has theoretical, practical, political, and ethical dimensions, it may be said that where women's studies goes, there are we all going."[91]

Notes

1. "Women's Studies News," Vol. 11, #4, Summer 1986, p. 3, and Ellen Langill interviews with Margo Anderson and Susan Burgess.

2. Suzanne P. Waller, Acting Director, "Planning Document: Center for Women's Studies, 1986–1991," p. 2.

3. A "curricular area number" is a prefix to course numbers indicating the unit (e.g., a department or program) sponsoring the course.

4. Waller, "Planning Document," p. 4.

5. "Main Activities and Accomplishments: Center for Women's Studies," 1992–1996, UW-Milwaukee Archives, p. 6.

6. "Main Activities and Accomplishments," UW-Milwaukee, p. 4. Personal communication, Susan Burgess to Laura Stempel Mumford, February 12, 1999.

7. Personal communication, Susan Burgess to Laura Stempel Mumford, February 12, 1999.

8. "Main Activities and Accomplishments," UW-Milwaukee.

9. "Main Activities and Accomplishments," UW-Milwaukee.

10. "Main Activities and Accomplishments," UW-Milwaukee.

11. Susan Burgess, Director, "Center for Women's Studies," Program Report, Program Array Review, November 1997.

12. Personal communication, Susan Burgess to Laura Stempel Mumford, February 12, 1999.

13. Ellen Langill interview with Susan Burgess; Burgess, Program Report.

14. Burgess, Program Report.

15. Personal communication, Susan Burgess to Laura Stempel Mumford, February 12, 1999.

16. Ellen Langill interview with Agate Nesaule (formerly Krouse).

17. Personal communication, Star Olderman to Laura Stempel Mumford, April 21, 1999.

18. Ellen Langill interviews with Star Olderman and Agate Nesaule.

19. Ellen Langill interview with Ruth Schauer.

20. Ellen Langill interview with Ruth Schauer.

21. "Honorary Fellow Program for Women's Studies Researchers Continues," in Women's Studies Consortium files; Ellen Langill interviews with Star Olderman, Agate Nesaule, Audrey Roberts, and Ruth Schauer.

22. The UW-Whitewater Women's Studies Minor Survey Results, January 1990, in Whitewater files, Consortium.

23. Ellen Langill interviews with Agate Nesaule, Ruth Schauer, and Star

Olderman; "Proposal for Authorization to Plan and Implement a New Academic Program—Bachelor of Arts and Bachelor of Science in Women's Studies," University of Wisconsin-Whitewater, October 1989, in Women's Studies Consortium files.

24. "Women Studies Department Annual Report, Whitewater, 1993," and "Activities Report 1992," in Women's Studies Consortium files.

25. "The Women's Studies Program Self-Study, July 1993," UW-Green Bay, p. 2.

26. "News from UW-Green Bay," 1983, in Women's Studies Consortium files.

27. Estella Lauter, "On Trying a Feminist's Soul," in Marian J. Swoboda, Audrey Roberts, and Jennifer Hirsh (eds.), *Women on Campus in the Eighties: Old Struggles, New Victories*, University Women: A Series of Essays (Madison: University of Wisconsin System Office of Women, 1993), Vol. IV, pp. 64–65; Ellen Langill interviews with Sidney Bremer, Julie Brickley, and Estella Lauter.

28. Letter from Sidney Bremer and Estella Lauter to Eugene P. Trani, May 19, 1988, in Women's Studies Consortium files.

29. Irene Kiefer, "Interdisciplinary Approach Pays off at UW-Green Bay," in Women's Studies Consortium files.

30. "The Women's Studies Program Self-Study," UW-Green Bay, p. 4.

31. "The Women's Studies Program Self-Study," UW-Green Bay, pp. 12, 13, in Women's Studies Consortium files. As noted in Chapter 4, the UW-Green Bay curriculum is organized around interdisciplinary "concentrations" rather than conventional departments.

32. "The Women's Studies Program Self-Study," UW-Green Bay, p. 23.

33. Ellen Langill interviews with Barbara Sniffen and Estella Lauter.

34. Ellen Langill interview with Barbara Sniffen.

35. Ellen Langill interview with Barbara Parsons; UW-Platteville "Women's Studies Newsletter," Spring 1998; Barbara Parsons, "Sedition in a Sexist Society: The Platteville Paradigm," in Marian Swoboda and Audrey Roberts (eds.), *Women Emerge in the Seventies*, University Women: A Series of Essays (Madison: University of Wisconsin System Office of Women, 1980), Vol. III, pp. 64–69.

36. Ellen Langill interviews with Barbara Parsons and Jacqueline Ross.

37. Ellen Langill interview with Barbara Parsons.

38. "Women's Studies Newsletter"; and Parsons, "Sedition in a Sexist Society."

39. "Women's Studies Newsletter," p. 2.

40. Ellen Langill interview with Carole Vopat.

41. Ellen Langill interview with Carole Vopat.

42. Ellen Langill interviews with Carol Lee Saffioti-Hughes, Frances M. Kavenik, Mary Kay Schleiter, Theresa Reinders, Evelyn Zepp, and Anne Statham.

43. Personal communication, Carole Vopat to Laura Stempel Mumford, August 30, 1998.

44. Personal communication, Frances M. Kavenik to Laura Stempel Mumford, August 30, 1998.

45. Ellen Langill interviews with Mary Kay Schleiter, Carol Lee Saffioti-Hughes, and Frances M. Kavenik.

46. Final Report, System Task Force on Women's Studies, September 30, 1974; Judith Green, "How It Worked on One Campus: Women's Studies at the University of Wisconsin-La Crosse."

47. Judith Green, "How It Worked on One Campus"; Ellen Langill interview with Sandra Krajewski.

48. Ellen Langill interview with Sandra Krajewski; Judith McCaslin, "Women and Education at UW-La Crosse: Recollections, Reflections, and Revision."

49. McCaslin, "Women and Education at UW-La Crosse." In *When Women Ask the Questions: Creating Women's Studies in America* (Baltimore: Johns Hopkins University Press, 1998), Marilyn Jacoby Boxer remarks on this common question: "If the originators of women's studies recognized any perils in naming, they were likely to have been concerned about accusations of a lack of objectivity or bias against men. 'Where are the men's studies?' was a more likely challenge in those days than 'Who do you mean by 'women'?'" (p. 13).

50. Ellen Langill interview with Sandra Krajewski.

51. "Women Centered," The Newsletter of the Institute for Women's Studies, UW-La Crosse, March 1981.

52. "Women Centered," March 1981.

53. Personal communication, Sandra Krajewski to Laura Stempel Mumford.

54. Ellen Langill interviews with Carol Fairbanks, Edna S. Hood, and Sarah Harder.

55. Personal communication, Edna S. Hood to Laura Stempel Mumford, September 13, 1998.

56. Ellen Langill interviews with Edna S. Hood, Carol Fairbanks, and Sarah Harder.

57. Personal communication, Edna S. Hood to Laura Stempel Mumford, September 13, 1998.

58. Bulletin of the Office of Public Information, University of Wisconsin-Eau Claire, February 16, 1978; Ellen Langill interviews with Carol Fairbanks and Edna S. Hood.

59. "Office of Public Information Bulletin," UW-Eau Claire, February 1, 1978.

60. Ellen Langill interview with Sarah Harder.

61. Ellen Langill interview with Sarah Harder.

62. "University News and Publications," UW-Eau Claire, February 21, 1978, and April 17, 1979.

63. Personal communication, Sarah Harder to Laura Stempel Mumford, February 22, 1999.

64. "News from UW-Eau Claire," in *Women's Studies Bulletin*, Fall 1982, p. 13; "Women in Transition, Project Summary," University of Wisconsin-Eau Claire, School of Arts and Sciences, March, 1995.

65. *Women in Transition: Perspectives from the Chippewa Valley* ("Myths and Stereotypes," "Taking the First Step," and "Snakes and Ladders") was produced by the Outreach Project on Women and the Economy, University of Wisconsin-Eau Claire, and deals with the benefits to women on welfare of higher education as a route to economic self-sufficiency.

66. Ellen Langill interview with Alice Randlett.

67. Ellen Langill interviews with Mary Jo Buggs and Alice Randlett.

68. Donna Garr, quoted in Kathy Ackley, "A New Direction for UW-Stevens Point," in Swoboda & Roberts (eds.), Vol. IV, p. 53.

69. Ackley, "A New Direction."

70. Ellen Langill interviews with Mary Jo Buggs and Nancy Bayne; "Women's Studies Program Review," UW-Stevens Point, April 27, 1995.

71. "Women's Studies Program Review," UW-Stevens Point, 1995.

72. "Women's Studies Program Review," UW-Stevens Point, 1995.

73. Ellen Langill interviews with Janet Polansky and Sharon Nero.

74. Ellen Langill interview with Fran Garb.

75. Ellen Langill interviews with Janet Polansky, Debra Nordgren, and Mary Richards. Timper's tenure denial "revolved around the image of several male faculty members in her Department of Social Sciences, that she was only dabbling in academic work and as the wife of a faculty member, was not to be taken seriously. Her denial was appealed but she lost the case; then she returned to graduate school to complete her Ph.D. degree, but did not return to the program at [UW-] Stout, nor did she continue her involvement in any of the women's studies activities." Personal communication, Ellen Langill to Laura Stempel Mumford, September 23, 1998.

76. Personal communication, Janet Polansky to Laura Stempel Mumford.

77. Ellen Langill interview with Janet Polansky.

78. Ellen Langill interview with Janet Polansky.

79. Ellen Langill interviews with Janet Polansky and Sharon Nero.

80. Personal communication, Janet Polansky to Laura Stempel Mumford.

81. Ellen Langill interviews with Janet Polansky, Fran Garb, and Sharon Nero.

82. Delores Harms, Memo to College of Education Vice Chancellor, November 9,

1976, in Women's Studies archives, UW-Superior.

83. "Women's Program Committee Minutes, October 18, 1976," UW-Superior, Women's Studies Archives.

84. Report of the UW System Conference, April 23, 1976 to Chancellor Edward Fort, of the UW Center System.

85. Personal communication, Jane Ewens (formerly Holbrook) to Laura Stempel Mumford, February 19, 1999.

86. Final Report, System Task Force on Women's Studies, 1974.

87. Laura Quinn, "Coming From Behind: Women's Studies at UW-River Falls," in Swoboda & Roberts, Vol. IV, pp. 57–60.

88. Quinn, "Coming from Behind"; Ellen Langill interviews with Kathy Tomlinson and Margaret Swanson.

89. Ellen Langill interviews with Kathy Tomlinson and Margaret Swanson; Quinn, "Coming from Behind," p. 60.

90. Elaine Marks, "Presentation to the Board of Regents, February 8, 1985."

91. Marks, "Presentation to the Board of Regents."

Chapter 8

The Women's Studies Consortium

By the late 1980s, with women's studies programs and departments on every campus of the University of Wisconsin System, the informal network of women's studies administrators still operated as a source of information and support and their semi-annual meetings offered opportunities for participants to share their experiences and collaborate on new projects. The office of the Women's Studies Librarian-at-Large (WSL) continued to support library resource and collection development on individual campuses, and produced bibliographies and other publications for both Wisconsin faculty and students, and for women's studies practitioners around the country. But when an opportunity presented itself for this informal organization to take on a new and more formal identity, members embraced it with enthusiasm.

In 1987, the University of Wisconsin System announced that it would create Centers of Excellence around the state to support institutional cooperation among campuses. The women's studies administrators saw the Centers for Excellence plan as a chance to formalize their long-standing association. Although the Centers were never funded, their proposal—the writing of which was supported by an Undergraduate Teaching Improvement Council (UTIC) grant—became the foundation of the UW System Women's Studies Consortium.

The initial proposal highlighted four areas as a focus for the women's studies center's first five years: 1) the creation of visiting professorships to foster collaborative work on specific women's issues; 2) a research incentive program; 3) a statewide clearinghouse for audio-visual materials in women's studies; and 4) an outreach program to bring women's studies to off-campus audiences.[1]

The women's studies administrators saw several key advantages to such a center, including a shift of the existing mainly volunteer structure into a funded organization with paid staff, and the ability to seek additional funding collectively to support programs for visiting scholars. They also hoped to design a Systemwide Women and Science Program, support additional integration of ethnic studies and racial diversity into the curriculum at campuses around the state, and hold a national conference on women's studies in prisons.[2]

As a committee of program administrators prepared the proposal, they drew on the history of statewide cooperation achieved first by the Wisconsin Coordinating Council for Women in Higher Education (WCCWHE), and then by the ongoing program administrators' group, to demonstrate that the University of Wisconsin already had a collective group of women's studies scholars and teachers working across the System to achieve excellence. With Cara Chell, a UW System academic planner, the committee—Margo Anderson (UW-Milwaukee), Jane Ewens (then Holbrook) (UW-Waukesha), Estella Lauter (UW-Green Bay),

Jacqueline Ross (UW-Platteville), and Sue Searing (Women's Studies Librarian-at-Large)—drafted a proposal that was circulated among the fourteen UW System institutions, seeking letters of support from the chancellors of each campus and a commitment to pledge $1,000 each to fund the startup of the formal Consortium.

As campus after campus signed on to the Center for Excellence proposal, a floodgate of revealing comments came forward with the letters of support. Campus women's studies administrators agreed that it was high time the work of the informal group got financial support from the UW System, and these messages also reflected the funding troubles that afflicted many women's studies programs in the state. Administrators' letters spoke of the many volunteer efforts put in by women's studies faculty on their home campuses, in addition to the numerous unpaid hours spent attending Systemwide meetings, where even travel expenses were often not reimbursed.

One coordinator noted, "Ours is a small program, run on a ridiculously small budget."[3] Another remarked that "This proposal gives us hope. We have struggled for years with minimum funding. In fact we have less funding per student than any other program or department on our campus. The establishment of a Center of Excellence in Women's Studies would allow us for the first time to have the increased funding we need to approach our potential."[4] When the final proposal was submitted, the budget included money for a half-time administrator, a part-time staff position, and some office and travel support—still at the level of bare-bones funding, but far more than had previously been available.[5]

In September, the women's studies proposal was approved by the Board of Regents as the only Systemwide Center for Excellence, but formal financial support for the Centers themselves never materialized because the legislature ultimately vetoed funding. Still, the idea of a System Women's Studies Consortium was so persuasive that the administrators drafted a new proposal and submitted a budget request to Eugene Trani, Vice President for Academic Affairs, for support from the UW System and from each individual campus. Before he would consider the proposal, however, Trani insisted on a self-study, including an outside evaluator's report on the past record of the informal network, and Myra Dinnerstein from the University of Arizona and the Southwest Institute for Research on Women (SIROW) was selected as the evaluator.

While her report highlighted the program administrators' existing cooperative network, she noted that "women's studies is presently at a critical juncture in the UW System." Despite its national leadership in areas such as research and in the creation of the Women's Studies Librarian position, Dinnerstein believed that the momentum was in danger of being lost because Wisconsin's women's studies programs had not had "the budgetary strength . . . to expand or to replenish faculty lost to death, retirements, or normal attrition . . . [and] still remains vulnerable." Dinnerstein also pointed out that the past successes of individual programs had depended largely "on the volunteer efforts of women's studies faculty who have undertaken those tasks in addition to their work on their campus women's studies programs and their regular faculty duties."[6]

In marshalling the effort to get financial support from the UW System, the women's studies administrators underscored that fact that they were "deeply concerned that the progress already made toward the realization of the Center's [Consortium's] goals not be hindered or lost because of a lack of funds for supplies, services, and personnel." They also emphasized their belief that the proposed Consortium had the potential to "bring national attention to the UW System."[7]

The proposed interim financial plan included stipends from each of the System campuses, and $5,000 in support from System Academic Affairs. In his letter to all of the Vice Chancellors, Trani underscored the fact that the campus contributions must "*not* be taken out of the budget of your campus's Women's Studies Program."[8] With the receipt of this interim funding and supplementary grants,[9] the Women's Studies Consortium, with Jacqueline Ross as its half-time interim director, began its operations in August, 1989, housed temporarily in what was then called UW Centers Administration in Madison, the site of Ross's office as director of the Postsecondary Re-Entry Education Program (PREP). Ross's appointment was based on her long record of service and leadership in women's studies. As a founder of the UW-Platteville Women's Studies Program, Ross had chaired it for almost a decade before taking a leave to establish and direct a college-degree-granting program for inmates in the Wisconsin State Prison System, originally funded through the federal Comprehensive Employment and Training Act (CETA) program.[10] While there, Ross had continued her active involvement with the network of women's studies administrators, attending the regular meetings and working on projects, conferences, and the proposal for the women's studies Center for Excellence.[11]

Another proposal for permanent funding of what was now the Women's Studies Consortium was submitted to the Board of Regents for inclusion in the 1991–93 biennial budget. When it was denied, Trani requested the renewal of the $1,000 yearly commitment from the campuses, reminding the Vice Chancellors that "integrating gender scholarship into the curriculum at all levels is itself a System priority,"[12] and reappointed Ross as Interim Director for the 1990–91 academic year. By the spring of 1991, Acting UW System President Katharine Lyall and new Vice President for Academic Affairs Stephen Portch had established a substantial budget that would support the hiring of a permanent Director for the Consortium. A search committee selected Jackie Ross for that position in the summer of 1991, with the Consortium to be housed in Academic Affairs.

Among the major accomplishments of the Consortium's first two years were the creation of an Audio-Visual Collection (housed at UW-Platteville), the establishment of a pilot Outreach program, collaborative efforts in the area of women and science, the incorporation of the Women's Studies Librarian's Advisory Panel under the Consortium's organizational structure, and the fall 1991 visit of women from the former Soviet Union (described later in this chapter).

* * * * *

While women's studies programs were being established and growing at the state's many campuses, Kay Clarenbach, Connie Threinen, and Marian Thompson had also built up the programming offered through UW-Extension, including Jane Schulenberg's history courses, Threinen's women's film series, an independent study course on women's health (created by Mariamne Whatley) and an introduction to women's studies (created by Virginia Sapiro).[13] The Extension staff had also offered Educational Telephone Network (ETN) classes on women and sports, women and the law, and women in communication, sponsored seminars on women and the arts and women in business management, and continued to sponsor the College Week for Women with courses increasingly attuned to women's issues and with women's studies content. Thompson, Threinen, and Clarenbach also still oversaw the School for Workers, begun in the 1930s, which provided seminars for women about union contracts, union organization, and federal labor legislation.[14] Another unique program reached out to Native American women and girls to offer experiences in gathering oral history from tribal elders, and to discuss the special issues facing tribal women and girls in the 1980s and 1990s.[15]

However, by 1989, the year in which the Consortium was founded, these three key Extension figures were ready to retire, and their outreach programs seemed to be in jeopardy. In her retirement note to the Consortium, Threinen reminded the administrators that "the outreach function is very important—if we are to keep the citizens conscious of women's studies and its importance [including] its need for continued funding, continued political effectiveness, etc." She also pointed out several valuable programs at Extension for women coaches and athletes, and for women policy makers within state government which, as she sadly noted, "will probably die unless someone else picks them up."[16]

Threinen's worries proved unnecessary, however, because from the beginning, the Women's Studies Consortium saw outreach as a central part of its mission, and the Associate Dean of General Extension was a permanent member of its Executive Committee. Working with Extension administrator Dolores Niles in the spring of 1990, the Consortium submitted a grant proposal to establish an ongoing outreach program. And in his letter supporting the original proposal for an Outreach component to be a part of the Women's Studies Consortium, Vice President Trani had described its function as exploring the "public policy implications of the new knowledge on gender issues [and bringing it] to the citizenry of Wisconsin." He believed that such a program had the potential to become a national model for outreach efforts on women's issues, "with broad implications for our economy and society over the coming decades."[17]

The three-year pilot for the Consortium Outreach program was funded in 1990 through a Curriculum and Development Program Initiative grant (CDPI), which created the new office of Consortium Outreach Administrator, a position held first by Betsy Hirsh, a graduate of the UW-Madison English department's doctoral program. The grant also included support to develop Consortium-sponsored programs, beginning with "Women and the Economy," with the theme "Self-Sufficiency for Women, Prosperity for All." During the pilot period, the Consortium was able to award grants to various System faculty for program development and delivery, and grants from $1,500 to $10,000 per campus could be used for instructional materials, publicity, honoraria, and video and equipment rental, with a conference planned for the fall of 1993 that would include an evaluation of the first three years of these outreach grants.[18] Since outreach offices already existed on every campus in the state through Extension, part of Hirsh's job was to bring women's studies into that network.

The new statewide Consortium Outreach Advisory Board included representatives from the State Vocational Board, the American Association of University Women (AAUW), the Wisconsin Women's Network, the Wisconsin Women's Council, the Wisconsin League of Municipalities, Milwaukee 9 to 5, and the Tribal Development Association of the Stockbridge-Muncie. Women's studies administrators with a long commitment to community outreach, including Sarah Harder (UW-Eau Claire), Anne Statham (UW-Parkside), and Nancy Worcester (Women's Studies Outreach Coordinator, UW-Madison), also worked with Hirsh to expand women's studies beyond traditional campus outlets.

Donna Silver followed Hirsh as Outreach administrator, continuing such projects as the annual Women and Science Days held on UW System campuses. She was succeeded in 1992 by Anne Statham, during whose tenure permanent funding for the office was established, and a number of ambitious long-term projects were begun. In addition to overseeing mini-grants awarded for local projects such as a UW-Oshkosh conference for re-entry women and a UW-River Falls study of how college students choose their majors, the Outreach office helped organize the ongoing annual System women's studies conferences, held on a different UW System campus each year. In 1994, the Women and Poverty Education Initiative began an eight-campus collaborative project involving Continuing Education Extension and women from the poverty community, and featuring workshops, surveys, and a series of interviews that led to the release of the 1996 report "In Our Own Words: Mothers' Perspectives on Welfare Reform," which received attention in national welfare circles.[19]

The Outreach office also developed a four-part certificate in Women's Leadership in Social Change, which included courses offered at UW-Eau Claire, Milwaukee, Madison and Parkside, with a follow-up conference with the Wisconsin Women's Network through a Women's Summit. The Wisconsin Indian Curriculum Project conducted twenty workshops on five campuses across the state, led by Wisconsin Indian specialists who assisted UW faculty in integrating material on Native American women into their courses.

As a follow-up to this project, the UW-Fond du Lac offered a series of workshops funded by the Wisconsin Humanities Commission on "Tribal Sovereignty," "Voices, Traditions, and Visions," and "Art, Traditions and Visions," and established a Web site to make the material more widely available. A 1998 international conference on Women and the Environment held at the Wingspread Conference Center in Racine demonstrated the ongoing Outreach commitment to environmental issues (expressed in the 1997 state women's studies conference) and to international women's issues. By 1998, nearly every campus had participated in these outreach programs, which brought many faculty, students, and community members together for a common purpose.[20]

* * * * *

One of the Women's Studies Consortium's most dramatic projects brought women from the former Soviet Union to Wisconsin in the fall of 1991, coincidentally just two weeks after the collapse of the USSR.[21] The origins of that project went back to the 1980s, and Sarah Harder, of the UW-Eau Claire, had played a significant role in an earlier Summit, held in New York and Washington, D.C., because of her role as president of the American Association of University Women (AAUW). Following that conference, two of the Soviet women—Ninel Maslova and Elvira Novikova—had visited Madison at Harder's invitation and met with several Consortium members, indicating their interest in learning about women's studies in the U.S. and "forging formal connections with the UW women's studies programs."[22]

Concrete plans for the exchange were finalized when Jackie Ross and Marian Swoboda, head of the UW System Office of Women, visited the Soviet Union in 1989. Women there had expressed interest in establishing academic women's studies programs similar to those in the United States, and Ross and Swoboda met with a wide range of women from fields such as engineering, the humanities, sciences, and education, and representing a variety of political allegiances. Additional contacts were made when Women's Studies Librarian Sue Searing visited Anastasiya Posadskaya, the director of the newly established Center for Gender Studies at the Academy of Sciences of the USSR in Moscow.

Eleven women were selected to participate in the UW program, but just before they were ready to depart for Wisconsin, the Soviet Union abruptly collapsed, and their U.S. hosts discovered that the precipitous decline in the value of the ruble had made the purchase of the last several airline tickets impossible. At. that time, Sarah Harder was in Moscow and Jackie Ross and her assistant Sylvia Ferronyoka had to scramble to save the project. They were able to raise the additional $800 from System Vice President Stephen Portch, but had no safe or legal way to get the money to Harder. They finally found two American women from Louisiana who were planning to depart shortly on a trip to Moscow and who agreed to carry the money to Harder, even though it was forbidden by the new

Russian government.[23] Ross wired the $800 to these two strangers, trusting that they would carry it safely, and Harder was able to buy the needed tickets in time for the Soviet group to depart on schedule.

The women finally arrived in Wisconsin on October 9. The program for the visiting scholars was funded in part by a grant from the Wisconsin Humanities Commission, with the assistance of the Johnson Foundation, whose Wingspread Conference Center in Racine was the site for a three-day opening conference involving people from throughout the UW System, as well as representatives from NCRW and other national organizations. United Nations translators assisted in sessions on topics such as "Models for Developing Women's Studies," "Women's Studies and Women's Lives," "Looking to the Future," and "Planning Together."[24] Over the next ten days, individual visitors toured more than twenty campuses around the System, and met with women's studies faculty, students, and community members, appeared at public forums, visited academic and non-academic programs such as women's shelters, and stayed in local homes.

UW-Milwaukee hosted the Consortium's annual fall Women's Studies Conference, at which the now-post-Soviet women were part of a panel with feminist leaders such as Judy Goldsmith (now Dean of UW-Fond du Lac) and Hannah Rosenthal, then the Executive Director of the Wisconsin Women's Council. The women's final activity was a visit to UW-Madison, including a public forum held at the Wisconsin Historical Society that drew more than 500 people.

Although the purpose of the visit was to exchange ideas about women's studies, memories of informal moments lingered with many of the Wisconsin participants. On one occasion during the Wingspread conference, for instance, women turned on a television set to watch part of the hearings on Clarence Thomas's controversial nomination to the U.S. Supreme Court. The issue of sexual harassment became a topic of discussion and Jackie Ross recalled the bewilderment among their visitors about the term, and their surprise that such behavior was a legal issue in the United States when it was simply a familiar part of work life for them.[25]

For the Consortium, this visit also had long-lasting impact, reinforced by ongoing activities, including additional visits by women's studies faculty and administrators to Russia. For some U.S. participants, the experience was a transformative one, leading to a new interest in international women's issues.

* * * * *

A demonstration of the far-reaching impact of a statewide organization of women's studies scholars and teachers came with the success of the Consortium's Women and Science program. Curriculum reform was an early and central focus across the state, and science was chosen as a major Consortium focus because of members' widespread concern that few women students chose science as a field, so that many opportunities and talents were lost. As Ethel Sloane, a biologist at UW-Milwaukee, stated, "If we can demystify science and medicine and explore the ways in which scientific knowledge is gained, we may be able to instill in our women students confidence in their own abilities."[26] In describing the origins of the Consortium's commitment to this project, Director Jackie Ross also credited a personal mentor, neuroanatomist Ruth Bleier, who had been an inspiration for many Wisconsin women. In addition to her efforts in encouraging women around the UW System to organize and lobby for women's studies and improvements in women's status, Bleier had been enormously influential in shaping a feminist critique of science.

National trends indicated that men were disproportionately represented among students receiving both undergraduate and graduate degrees, leading ultimately to a severe shortage of women faculty in the sciences. As Ross pointed out, "We were concerned about stories we had heard about the hostile climate in the sciences affecting women faculty, staff, and students . . . In light of this resistance, it is not surprising that we encountered barriers from many faculty in the sciences as we developed the program in their territory."[27] Ross noted that "the intent of the Consortium's Executive Committee was to create a model program for curricular transformation of the sciences in the UW System that could be replicated or adapted by other universities and colleges, large and small, public and private, nationwide." Its primary focus initially was to reverse the pattern of attrition of women and minority students from science, mathematics, and engineering courses, and startup funding from the Undergraduate Teaching Improvement Council (UTIC) allowed the early program planning to go forward.

The funding for the Women and Science Project came in 1992, from the Undergraduate Education Division of the National Science Foundation (NSF), with grants eventually reaching nearly one million dollars. The project began with an opening conference, whose keynote address on the reasons such curriculum transformation designs were crucial was delivered by Sheila Tobias—the editor of *Female Studies*, the first collection of women's studies syllabi published in 1970, as well as an authority on undergraduate science programs. This initial conference brought together faculty from throughout the UW System to discuss ways of improving the quality of education in the sciences through workshops, conferences, retreats, and other activities. Discussions centered on new gender-sensitive strategies for improving the curriculum, pedagogical approaches, and climate in the science classroom.[28]

The Women and Science Project's main structure involved bringing Distinguished Visiting Professors (DVPs) from both inside and outside of the UW System for semester-long stays at individual campuses, in order to demonstrate "hands on" programs in science courses that would address the attrition problems. A typical assignment for such a visiting professor was to teach a model introductory course, hold faculty development seminars on the incorporation of race- and gender-sensitive content into courses, and work closely with members of science departments on the host campus to develop new course materials and syllabi. Faculty Fellows on each campus were then expected to develop and teach such a revised science course within two years.[29]

As the project's first DVP, biology professor Ethel Sloane—one of UW-Milwaukee's first women's studies faculty members—offered a course in the "Biology of Women" at UW-Waukesha. Although the course was initially not publicized sufficiently, at the last minute, fliers were circulated, the course filled to capacity, and evaluations were overwhelmingly positive. Students in Sloane's course credited it with changing their minds about majoring in science and she was described as a positive role model for students considering work in the field. Program evaluators Gloria Rogers and Judith Levy reported that "because of this program, faculty generally recognized a need to change the way they taught science and to examine their own teaching style."[30]

Another DVP, Cheryl Ney, a chemist at Capital University in Columbus, Ohio, acknowledged that few people in the academy understood the challenge of bringing a feminist critique to science. Most people were unaware, she noted, that women had been virtually excluded as subjects of health research prior to the 1970s, and did not realize how women's perspectives could help to explain natural phenomena. Ney's work with a Collaborative Community program, in which the campuses of UW-Eau Claire, River Falls, and Stout worked together on curriculum reform and faculty development activities, was seen as particularly effective.[31] Other highly successful DVPs included Sue Rosser (now Dean of the humanities and social sciences unit of the Georgia Institute of Technology), who had taught in the Women's Studies Program at UW-Madison in its early years. Rosser visited nine different UW System campuses in one semester, while Sharon Nichol, a mathematician at UW-Platteville, taught semester-long courses on several others.

Funding from the NSF was renewed for two more years, and the program continued to develop and reform science courses on UW System campuses through the application of "female-friendly" pedagogy, and, even more important, the development of women and science communities within and among institutions. Quoting Sheila Tobias, who returned to speak on the UW-Madison campus in October of 1997, Ross noted that "what works well for female students will also work well with intelligent, scientifically-inclined male students who drop out of these fields because of the ways in which it is characteristically taught."[32]

The NSF-funded project ended in 1996, and the Women and Science Program became a permanent part of the Women's Studies Consortium, housed at UW-Oshkosh and supported with money from the Vice Chancellors of all the UW System campuses. Physicist Heidi Fencl was hired as its Director, and the dual emphasis on faculty development and curriculum reform continued with year-round activities, including annual national Women and Science Institutes, with faculty from universities and colleges across the country working on projects involving pedagogy, curriculum, and climate.[33] The facilitators for the institutes have included faculty who had previously served as DVP's or Faculty Fellows in the Women and Science program.[34]

> *I am sure we have all heard the analogy that getting faculty members to agree on anything is like herding cats. Imagine the challenge when the cats are spread over 26 different campuses! Yet remarkably, the Women and Science Program actively includes educators from every UW institution, and the numbers are growing. Scientists and mathematicians in the UW System are recognizing that excellence in teaching promotes diversity in the classroom, and that attention to diversity improves education for all students. By maintaining a Systemwide Women and Science community, and by supporting the use of gender-conscious pedagogies in the classroom, the Program addresses the need for more women and students of color to pursue scientific study.*
>
> —Heidi Fencl

* * * * *

During the second ten years of women's studies programs in Wisconsin, the services of the Women's Studies Librarian (WSL) remained crucial. Helping to nurture the younger programs, strengthen the ties between the campuses, and publish resource lists were only a few of the significant contributions of the position. Sue Searing, the third WSL, noted that this framework of cooperation was not the norm in most university systems. More often new programs competed with each other for money and attention, but women's studies at the University of Wisconsin had become a model of how inter-institutional cooperation could enhance the experience on every campus.[35]

In the fall of 1990, Searing helped to create a new Advisory Panel for the Women's Studies Librarian's Office, which now reported directly to the Consortium. Before she left the position to take an administrative post, Searing organized a feminist film festival in Madison and worked to move the WSL office to a larger space on the fourth floor of the Memorial Library.[36]

An interim appointment brought Phyllis Holman Weisbard to the position beginning in 1991, and she was chosen as the permanent Women's Studies Librarian in 1994. Weisbard continued the bibliographic work begun by her predecessors. The many publications of the WSL's office continued to put Wisconsin in the forefront nationally and even internationally as a leader in women's studies information resources. Weisbard and Rima D. Apple compiled a new edition of the bibliography, *History of Women and Science, Health, and Technology*, and the office published *WAVE: Women's Audiovisuals in English: A Guide to Nonprint Resources in Women's Studies*, both in 1993. That year, in conjunction with the Advisory Panel, she also prepared a self-study of the Women's Studies Librarian's Office that found widespread support for the existing publication program and other services and looked ahead to increasing use of new technologies, both to distribute the office's publications and to access information created by others.[37]

Through the next several years Weisbard concentrated on making more of the women's studies resource information available electronically. She successfully negotiated for the inclusion of *New Books on Women & Feminism* and the bibliographies mentioned above in a commercial database, *Women's Resources International*, that debuted in 1996. The contract stipulated that any System campus could subscribe to the database at a greatly reduced price, bringing the cost down to an affordable level, and most campus libraries chose to subscribe. In this way the participation of the WSL publications in this composite database consisting of several important women's studies indexes brought an excellent research tool to campuses that in most cases would have been unable to offer it to their faculty and students. Royalty income also allowed the office to purchase better computers and software that increased the efficiency of producing the publications. Similarly, *Feminist Collections: A Quarterly of Women's Studies Resources* became part of two commercial full-text databases, *Contemporary Women's Issues* and *Women "R"* (later called *GenderWatch*).

Weisbard mounted many of the WSL bibliographies and selections from other publications on the Internet, first using Gopher technology and later the World Wide Web. Access to these resources went up immediately. In 1994, for example, some 6,000 people reviewed parts of *History of Women and Science, Health, and Technology* online. In 1996 Weisbard developed a web page for the WSL office that included bibliographies, articles from *Feminist Collections*, the catalog of the UW System Women's Studies Audiovisual Collection, topical core lists of women's studies books, and scores of subject-arranged annotated links to resources elsewhere. The opening page was accessed more than 12,250 times that first year and about 19,400 times in 1997. The prominence of the WSL's participation in the creation of both women's studies databases and Internet resources led to Weisbard being invited to present a talk on "Promoting Women's Studies Online" at the annual convention of the American Library Association, which she gave in June, 1996.[38]

Along with serving as the selector of women's studies materials for the Memorial Library collection, Weisbard continued the important tradition of visiting programs on campuses throughout the System, giving workshops and discussing program issues and needs. As the new technologies became available, these campus visits involved training local faculty in effective use of electronic resources and appropriate ways to incorporate them into classes. Besides demonstrating specific strategies, she discussed gender issues in the online environment, and also helped instructors find ways to prevent plagiarism from Internet sources.[39]

Because it remained nationally unique as a Systemwide position, the Women's Studies Librarian's office enhanced the visibility and the reputation of Wisconsin's women's studies programs. Weisbard found herself often involved in both national and international conferences, speaking about the Wisconsin experience and about the many resources developed by the WSL's office, which were increasingly available for world-wide usage.[40] Both students and faculty in women's studies programs throughout the state continued to benefit from the services of the WSL, as it celebrated its twentieth year of service in 1997.

* * * * *

As the decade of the 1990s drew to a close, the Women's Studies Consortium continued to explore ways of expanding the field's purview into new areas. A 1998 pilot project involving five UW System campuses represented an effort to use technology as a way of making a wide variety of women's studies courses available to students around the state. The proposed collaborative programming, coordinated by a committee of women's studies administrators, was created to allow students on the campuses of UW-Stevens Point, Platteville, Parkside, Whitewater, and UW Colleges to take courses together through distance education, using compressed video and other technologies to teach courses like women and science simultaneously in more than one UW System institution. The programming originally centered on these five campuses, but is being expanded to campuses throughout the UW System. Although the initial experience was difficult and illuminated the different cultures existing on each UW campus, the project also made it clear that women's studies continues to be innovative and to challenge traditional modes of delivery.[41]

During this same period, issues of hiring and retention continued to absorb the attention of many involved in the Consortium, along with the importance of increasing the number of women in administration and the future of interdisciplinary programs within the System. And despite the great expansion of courses and degrees over the previous 25 years, the curriculum transformation that had always been central to women's studies—the "continuing struggle to integrate women's concerns into the mainstream of higher education"—also remained of crucial significance.[42]

New challenges involved the effort to make women's studies more diverse in both its course offerings and its student, faculty, and staff—a complex problem for women's studies throughout its history, since the habit of dividing issues into those of concern primarily to people of color and those of concern primarily to women tends to leave women of color, who fall into both categories, feeling excluded everywhere. During the 1980s and 1990s, the UW System expanded its commitment to these issues through its Design for Diversity (1988) and Plan 2008 (1998),[43] and the Consortium reiterated its own longstanding recognition of the difficulty of even defining the basic terms: "Diversity simply in terms of race and/or culture is insufficient, since over fifty percent of those populations under consideration are female, and to address diversity without inclusion of this difference is not diversification at all," Outreach administrator Anne Statham wrote in connection with the Consortium's adoption of a formal policy in this area: "It would be a waste to fail to include this [women's studies] scholarship while accomplishing the goals of the Design for Diversity [since] the discipline of Women's Studies here at home and around the world has a long history of including in our scholarship and curriculum the study of women around the world, not just English speaking, Euro-centric women, but women of all races and cultural backgrounds."[44]

Nevertheless, both the Design for Diversity and its follow-up, Plan 2008, defined "diversity" exclusively in terms of racial and ethnic identity, prompting women's studies administrators and others around the state to propose a new, parallel initiative that would address the concerns of women throughout the UW System. In October 1998, President Katharine C. Lyall established a year-long, Systemwide Initiative on the Status of Women that in many ways brought the history of women's higher education in Wisconsin full-circle. The Initiative included two Systemwide ad hoc committees of faculty, staff, and students, staffed by a part-time director, Laura Stempel Mumford, and a program assistant.

The Committee on the Status of Women undertook a study of the experiences of women students, staff, faculty, and administrators throughout the System—the first one since the 1981 report of the Regents' Task Force—conducting a survey and campus focus groups, collecting statistical data, and doing other research in order to evaluate and make recommendations for improving the status of women students and employees. A separate Steering Committee organized a pilot Summer Leadership Institute, held in July, 1999, designed to begin to address one widely recognized gap: the lack of women and minority members in senior administration. At the end of the Initiative, the committees presented President Lyall with reports that suggested an ongoing evaluation of UW System women's needs and experiences, and made recommendations for remedies to specific problems.

Notes

1. Eugene P. Trani, "UW System Women's Studies Consortium, A Historical Overview related to Interim Funding," March 15, 1989, in Consortium files, Madison.

2. Eugene P. Trani, Letter to System Vice Chancellors, on the Progress of UW System Center of Excellence in Women's Studies, November 23, 1988, in Women's Studies Consortium files.

3. Teresa Peck, Letter to Eugene P. Trani (undated), in Women's Studies Consortium files.

4. Gloria Stephenson, Letter to Eugene P. Trani April 21, 1988, in Women's Studies Consortium files.

5. Ellen Langill interviews with Margo Anderson and Jacqueline Ross.

6. Dr. Myra Dinnerstein, "Executive Summary, the UW System Women's Studies Consortium Self-Study," in Women's Studies Consortium Files.

7. Women's Studies Consortium Executive Committee, Letter to Eugene P. Trani, March 15, 1989, in Women's Studies Consortium files.

8. Eugene P. Trani, Letter to Vice Chancellors, March 20, 1989, in Women's Studies Consortium files, Madison.

9. In addition to campus and System funding, the Consortium's early budget was supplemented with a $30,000 UTIC grant, and an administration match for a Fund for the Improvement of Postsecondary Education (FIPSE) grant for visiting professorships in a Women and Science program. Other funding in this period included UW-Extension support for Women and Science Days. Ellen Langill interview with Jacqueline Ross.

10. Rhonda Ambuehl and Barbara Sniffen, "Women's Studies in Prison: Lessons for Offenders, Lessons for Educators," in Marian Swoboda, Audrey Roberts, and Jennifer Hirsh (eds.), *Women on Campus in the Eighties: Old Struggles, New Victories*, University Women: A Series of Essays (Madison: University of Wisconsin System Office of Women, 1993), Vol. IV, pp. 69–78.

11. Ellen Langill interview with Jacqueline Ross.

12. Eugene P. Trani, Letter to Vice Chancellors, March 20, 1990, in Women's Studies Consortium files.

13. Ellen Langill interview with Marian Thompson; "Women's Studies, Extension and Outreach," brochure, in Women's Studies Consortium files.

14. "Women's Studies, Extension and Outreach," brochure.

15. Ellen Langill interview with Marian Thompson; "Women's Studies, Extension and Outreach," brochure.

16. Connie Threinen, Note to Susan Kahn, March 1, 1989, in Women's Studies Consortium files.

17. Eugene P. Trani, Letter to John Schmidt, Dean General Extension Division, UW-Extension, February 28, 1990, in Women's Studies Consortium files.

18. Elizabeth Hirsh, "Basic Facts About Consortium-Sponsored Outreach," in Women's Studies Consortium files.

19. University of Wisconsin System Women's Studies Consortium Outreach Office, Self-Study for Assessment, March, 1998; personal communication, Anne Statham to Laura Stempel Mumford, November 9, 1998.

20. Personal communication, Anne Statham to Laura Stempel Mumford, February 4, 1999.

21. "Just Peace: Disarmament to Daycare," Women for Meaningful Summits, Winter, 1991, in Women's Studies Consortium files.

22. Susan E. Searing, "Report on the Cooperative Activities between Women's Studies Practitioners in the United States and the Soviet Union," Report to the Consortium, August 28, 1990.

23. Ellen Langill interview with Jacqueline Ross.

24. "UW–USSR Women's Studies Conference: Wingspread October 10–12, 1991, Agenda."

25. Ellen Langill interview with Jacqueline Ross.

26. Ethel Sloane, as quoted by Jacqueline Ross in "Introduction," in Laura Stempel Mumford, Cheryl Ney, and Jacqueline Ross (eds.), *Flickering Clusters: Lessons from a Collaborative Science Curriculum Transformation Project* (under review).

27. Jacqueline Ross, "Introduction."

28. Ellen Langill interview with Jacqueline Ross; Ross, "Introduction."

29. Ross, "Introduction."

30. Ross, "Introduction."

31. Ross, "Introduction."

32. Sheila Tobias, *The Second Tier*, as quoted in Ross, "Introduction."

33. Ellen Langill interview with Heidi Fencl.

34. Ellen Langill interviews with Jacqueline Ross and Heidi Fencl.

35. Sue Searing, quoted by Karen Merritt, in "A Braid of Associations: Ten Years of Women's Studies in Wisconsin," *Frontiers,* vol. 8 #3 (1986), p. 20.

36. "Advisory Panel to the UW System Women's Studies Librarian," Meeting, May 18, 1990, in Women's Studies Consortium files.

37. Ellen Langill interview with Phyllis Holman Weisbard; "1994 Performance Report, Women's Studies Librarian," Submitted January 3, 1995.

38. Phyllis Holman Weisbard, "1993, WSL Self-Study," "1995 Activities Summary," "Activities and Accomplishments for 1996 and 1997."

39. Weisbard, "1993, WSL Self-Study," "1995 Activities Summary," "Activities and Accomplishments for 1996 and 1997."

40. Weisbard, "1993, WSL Self-Study," "1995 Activities Summary," "Activities and Accomplishments for 1996 and 1997."

41. Ellen Langill interview with Star Olderman.

42. Jacqueline Ross, Letter to Theodore J. Marchese, American Association for Higher Education, May 3, 1990, Women's Studies Consortium files.

43. The Design for Diversity was a 10-year project aimed at improving the representation of students, faculty, and staff of color throughout the UW System—the first university-wide plan of this kind in the U.S. Goals included enlarging the populations of those targeted groups, as well as developing partnerships between the University and both pre- and post-college programs in the community. In 1998, the UW System instituted Plan 2008, a new 10-year initiative designed to fill the remaining gaps in recruitment and retention of students, staff, and faculty of color. See "Plan 2008: Educational Quality Through Racial and Ethnic Diversity," University of Wisconsin System, May 1998.

44. Anne Statham, Memo to Jacqueline Ross, "Consortium Position Statement on Inclusion of Material about Women in Diversity Courses."

Conclusion

Just as in the mid-19th century, when women were first admitted to what was then the University of Wisconsin, questions persist today about their acceptance as full members of the university community. Are women represented as faculty, staff, and administrators in numbers that reflect their majority status as students? Are their needs for services, curriculum, and career opportunities being met? Do they continue to face discrimination, harassment, and other obstacles because of their identities as women?

While the questions sound familiar, the context for them has of course changed—as the history described in the preceding eight chapters makes clear. Unlike the handful of women admitted solely to teacher-education courses in the early 1860s, women students, who now form a majority within the System, can get degrees in any field, and can find women mentors and role models in almost every facet of university life. Every campus within the UW System has a women's studies program or department, and a Systemwide Consortium serves as a network that helps women's studies faculty, staff, and administrators deal with the challenges of curriculum, budget, personnel, and university politics. And perhaps the most visible sign of change is the fact that a woman President stands at the head of the statewide institution, a far cry from the days—not so many years ago—when some campuses had few women even as full professors, and deans were able to refuse to consider the possibility of a woman chairing a department.

> When Sheila Kaplan was chosen as UW-Parkside's first woman Chancellor, women faculty, staff, and students had great hopes for her tenure. Minimally, they expected to be heard in ways that they had not previously been heard, or seen as valued members of the UW-Parkside community. And indeed, over the next few years, a number of questions were asked—about women's studies, women staff and students, and sexual harassment—that turned into campuswide initiatives with real consequences. As Chancellor, Sheila Kaplan gave us a solid foundation from which to launch our own careers, scholarship, teaching innovations, community action, and advocacy. She also showed us how wit, style, and strength could combine to make a women leader one could be proud to follow.
>
> — Frances M. Kavenik

Still, despite those truly revolutionary changes in women's status, women's studies itself continues to struggle for respect and funding, with the programs at smaller campuses often operating on tiny budgets that demand hours of voluntary overtime from dedicated faculty and staff. The curriculum transformation concept at the heart of women's studies is far from complete, and feminist scholars associated with the field must still often argue for the serious nature of their work against colleagues who continue to see it as "trendy." In an era of tight budgets and an increasingly difficult academic job market, those who specialize in women's studies can find themselves professionally marginalized and even unemployed, and with more students concerned about the practical use of their ever more expensive and time-consuming degrees, the question "What can you do with a B.A. in women's studies?" assumes real urgency.

Nevertheless, when women's studies practitioners and supporters convene their 25th annual statewide conference at the UW-Madison in the fall of the year 2000, they'll have a lot to celebrate. The stability of the University of Wisconsin's fourteen women's studies programs and departments, and of the UW System Women's Studies Consortium, represent a triumph of hard work and commitment over financial, political, and career-related obstacles that could easily have derailed a less dedicated cadre of faculty, students, and staff. As women's studies in Wisconsin enters the 21st century, those who have built and sustained it can be proud of an accomplishment that makes the UW System unique, and that continues to contribute to the strength of the field.